Last of the Summer Wickets

Tales from the Scarborough Cricket Festival

John Fuller

Foreword by Sir Michael Parkinson

GREAT NORTHERN

Great Northern Books
PO Box 1380, Bradford,
West Yorkshire, BD5 5FB

www.greatnorthernbooks.co.uk

ISBN: 978-1-912101-21-4

Cover illustration and design by Moira Fuller
Layout by David Burrill

CIP Data
A catalogue for this book is available from the British Library

For Moira, who always believes in me

Award-winning journalist and author, John Fuller has been writing about cricket for more than two decades. He showcases the recreational game on cricketyorkshire.com and has written for *The Cricketer Magazine*, *Wisden Almanack* and *The Cricket Paper*. John was the winner of the JM Kilburn Award for Cricket Writer of the Year for his first book, *All Wickets Great and Small*.

For more information about John Fuller and his books, visit cricketyorkshire.com

Contents

Foreword

My introduction to the Scarborough Cricket Festival was when I was 14 and peeling potatoes at the Grand Hotel. My uncle Bernard was the chef and he arranged a holiday stint where he worked. It was a posh hotel in those days, and I remember peeking at the grand staircase as all the toffs and their begowned and bejewelled ladies made their entrance to the dining room.

Little did I know that a lifetime later I'd be President of the Cricket Festival with my own cricket XI, including players like Mark Waugh, Gordon Greenidge, Viv Richards, Michael Holding, Imran Khan, Wasim Akram, Joel Garner, Curtly Ambrose, to mention but a few.

They were halcyon days presided over by Don Robinson, who was an enthusiastic supporter of the Festival, as well as supplying the teams with a particularly potent vodka which he had imported from some distant Balkan state.

But it was serious cricket with individual performances counting in the first-class averages. After a morning spent lolloping in at three-quarter pace, the captain of my team, Wasim Akram, was not the devastating quick bowler I was looking for.

At lunch, I enquired as to his general health and

disposition, pointing out the opposition had lost only one wicket before lunch and were cruising. Ever charming, Wasim said he wasn't going to risk being flat out in a game which didn't count in the first-class averages.

When I convinced him that the opposite was true, he returned to the field after lunch as a man inspired and ripped through a decent MCC team captained by Roger Knight. Later, Roger asked me if I could account for Wasim's transformation.

'A mystery,' I said.

I used to go to the Festival as a kid, residing in a boarding house opposite the ground where the landlady kicked us out and wouldn't let us back in until 5pm.

It didn't matter when the Festival was on and the sun shone, but when it rained we would spend our holiday sitting in bus shelters or losing money in an amusement arcade. Later on, I played at Scarborough when my Barnsley team played the locals.

I opened with my dear friend, Dickie Bird, who continued playing for Yorkshire at Scarborough and beyond for a few seasons before he became the best-known and beloved umpire of the lot.

Nowadays, I seek out Dickie at the Festival and we have the best of times talking about what we got up to in our youth. Two old men nodding off in deck chairs, nursing happy memories, waiting for our time to bat in an altogether different place.

Sir Michael Parkinson

First-class cricket on holiday

Ticket number 01929 is khaki green and has sat on my office desk since the day I acquired it.

PASS OUT TICKET is printed on thick card in a crisp, black, bold font with 'SCARBOROUGH CRICKET CLUB' in the same typeface.

On the back, the message that 'Play is not guaranteed' and 'no money refunded' lends further weight to the whiff of the traditional. In our age of tweets and noses attached to our phones, scrolling away addictively, this is an old-school, collector's item.

It is, of course, the stub that county cricket fans receive if they dip out of the North Marine Road cricket ground but want to gain entry later. To me, it is as valuable as Willy Wonka's golden ticket.

It's not just that this pass out ticket has an indeterminate age and is satisfyingly of another lifetime. It's the promise of more cricket locked away in its oblong body once you've gone for your poke of chips and strolled Scarborough's North Bay promenade.

It's the opportunity to watch Yorkshire County Cricket

Club away from their Headingley headquarters, swapping a Test match stadium in a suburb of Leeds for an adventure on the shores of a seaside resort founded by Vikings.

Part of the joy of watching professional cricket in Scarborough is that you wouldn't know it was there. Encased in tenement housing, the ground is as far removed from the neon lights and jazz hands presence of a modern, sporting hub as you can get. It's not exactly a closely-guarded secret, but there's this abiding sense of community like an epic, underground house party.

My Scarborough Cricket Festival tales will be no bells-and-whistles history lesson, choosing instead to focus on the present coastal cricket carnival and drawing upon the stories and memories of county cricket fans, players and supporters who have come to North Marine Road over the years.

The Scarborough Cricket Festival has prospered and endured, the war years notwithstanding, since 1876, so there is much material to draw upon. It boasts a pedigree that saw this town punch above its weight by attracting the finest players ever to have graced the game from Bradman to Tendulkar and Hutton to Trueman.

Since my first visit, it has pulled on the heartstrings and is talked about across Yorkshire reverentially. Old men with flinty stares notably soften at the mention of Scarborough as a dear friend they've always got time for. County action from Scarborough has a life and pace of its own that is as alluring as anywhere I've had the privilege to watch a game of cricket.

As we'll get to hear, many plan their entire lives around cricket at Scarborough. It matters that much. It's a four-day drama played out annually in a Colosseum. Cricket on the North Yorkshire coast is treasured and has the Yorkshire equivalent of UNESCO World Heritage status.

The Festival's an institution that's had to adapt as decades swept by but has retained its charm by not changing too much. It achieves that by being itself. What embodies the appeal of Scarborough Cricket Club? How has the Festival changed in the last 50 years? Where are the best chips?

The centrepiece of this book will be the 2018 Festival; to revel in the quirks and idiosyncrasies and meet those for whom it is an essential passport stamp of their summer.

By the end, I want you to feel as if you'd had the sand between your toes, a mint choc chip melting down your hand and the cacophony of a Scarborough cricket crowd ringing in your ears. There will be plenty of original interviews garnered over a year, from Geoffrey Boycott to Darren Lehmann, but just as key are the moments that Yorkshire cricket fans shared with me.

As I begin this book, typing away on the keyboard on a Sunday morning mid-March, Yorkshire's first match of the 2018 season is three weeks away.

Outside, the West Yorkshire countryside is akin to a scene from the concluding Winter Olympics in PyeongChang, but Yorkshire County Cricket Club's first County Championship match against defending Champions Essex is inked for the inauspicious date of

(Friday) April 13.

The Siberian winds have returned to the UK and driven down temperatures below zero in what has been unimaginatively coined the 'Mini Beast from the East' after its more spiteful and disruptive predecessor.

Wearing a woolly hat, encased in a blanket and glancing with a degree of concern at the plucky oil heater that has yet to transform the office from a freezer box, another English cricket season is near and yet so far.

However, county cricket's return in April is a thought to warm the cockles, if not entirely nurture the circulation, and the countdown to the next Scarborough Cricket Festival is well underway.

This is the story of a love affair with a famed Yorkshire cricket institution across generations. County cricket at Scarborough is to step back in time or at the very least freeze it. Its popularity is nothing short of spectacular. So, pack your beach towel and dig out the sunscreen, we're off to the seaside!

On your marks, get set, the fixtures are out!

The day the county cricket fixtures are revealed each winter is a seismic moment for those of us who care about such things. For me, it heralds a change as profound as the first green buds of Spring or the clocks changing. The prospect of domestic cricket is suddenly tangible again.

Hoteliers in Scarborough steel themselves for their phone lines to melt; journalists dissect the calendar for quirks or controversy and supporters are able to untangle the logistics around getting from Colwyn Bay to Nottingham.

When the day arrived, meaningful work was impossible. I drank more tea than should be anatomically possible. I rearranged the mayhem of scattered, unattended papers across my office desk into an orderly pile of unattended papers.

It was November 29, 2017, and like thousands of others, I was waiting for 11am to tick round to herald the official countdown to the 2018 domestic season, as the fixtures were released by the England & Wales Cricket Board (ECB).

It was about 10.50am when I happened to jump onto my email and spotted an embargoed press release from Yorkshire County Cricket Club (permitted for publication shortly). It announced: 'Yorkshire to open against champions Essex.'

This gave me a window of ten minutes before the general public began booking every bed and breakfast, hostel, pub, flat or hotel in Scarborough. Cue absolute and total meltdown in the Fuller household.

It had been drummed into me that many fans, for whom a trip to revel in county cricket at Scarborough is as well-oiled a routine as breathing, don't even ring to confirm their hotels, but just leave the voicemail message: 'When the fixtures come out, book me in!' Forget a concert that sells out in minutes, this is the equivalent of the next concert being sold out the second the lights go out on the current one.

In the event of a lack of options, I envisaged having to hunker down in a sleeping bag on the beach or sneaking onto the cricket square and catching a few hours, protected by the overhang of the roll-on covers.

I had, at least, done some advanced research using the travel reviews website, TripAdvisor, to get a feel for the range of places I might stay; sensing that this temporary home may become as much a character in the book as the cricket.

I don't recall when I became worryingly obsessed with posting TripAdvisor reviews of cafes and restaurants as a writing antidote to wickets and runs across Yorkshire. If you're not careful, you spend most of the time photographing food then applying artistic tints on your mobile phone; documenting the moment rather being in it.

The gamification of our travel and eating experiences through being awarded badges for posting photos, writing reviews and generally being helpful has clearly appealed to my competitive nature.

I have put in countless hours in the pursuit of becoming a Top Contributor. Why? Well, you may well ask as there is no reward, discount or life-affirming 'eureka' moment; notwithstanding the notion of communal karma from sharing experiences online to help others.

This journalistic travel bitcoin dedication also ensures it's my go-to resource for booking a hotel or checking out a new destination for advice on where to get Persian cuisine at 5pm on a Thursday in Bradford or the relative merits of gluten-free cakes in Hebden Bridge.

Initial exploration revealed that Scarborough is nothing if not catering for both ends of the budget spectrum. I was keen to avoid hotel chains, believing that B&Bs would feel less impersonal and might be fertile ground for conversations relating to both cricket and the town.

Properties are ranked based on feedback and the top 20 were all unavailable for this chunk of August. That meant being open to exploring some of the more colourful and risky.

Each search result has a section for 'Professional Photos' where the hotelier or B&B owner can wow you with steaming plates of crispy bacon and fluffy pillows made from the wingspan of angels. It was quite remarkable how many photos were not of the place at all but of the sea, the beach, the comedian Ken Dodd, a McDonald's sign in one instance and most bizarre of all, a picture of a police car.

There is a common tactic with sales, based on psychological research, that has considerable success on us consumers: scarcity.

That is the idea that we're all more likely to buy something if we know it has limited availability. In those ten minutes before the Scarborough Cricket Festival dates became common knowledge, I clicked frantically around, fingers flitted over the keyboard and I Googled as if my life depended on it.

In 0.74 seconds, 739,000 search results filled my screen for 'Scarborough B&B' and while I navigated a booking website, it became apparent that it was a master at scarcity and cranking up the pressure.

Guest house entries were lit up in jarring red font by the number of times it had been booked in the last six hours. If that wasn't enough, subtle prompts to take action, such as 'in high demand' or 'if you don't book now, your life will never be the same again', inflated the sense of drama.

North Bay Guest House was rated as 'exceptional', which didn't strike me as something anyone in Yorkshire would call themselves, but was certainly good enough for me. An orange label which shouted 'Great Value Today' in no way swayed my online decision. Honest.

At the moment of making a final decision, the

knowledge that there was only one room left might, just might, have got me in a blind panic. The ensuing conversation with my ever-patient wife, Moira, went something like this:

'WE'RE DOOMED! WE'RE ALL DOOMED!'

'It will be fine. Where's your bank card?'

'NOOOOOOO! I'VE LOST MY CARD.'

'It's there. There. No, there. In front of you. The plastic thing with numbers on it.'

'Ah. It is indeed. Fancy that.'

Hyperventilating while trying to type my bank card number aside, the subsequent, satisfying confirmation pat on the back announced that we were all set for Scarborough.

There was no faulting the proximity to North Marine Road for the cricket, nor the exotic address of Columbus Ravine.

I felt buoyed by a couple's gushing review about the fruit salad at breakfast. Food and drink featured prominently in my last book travelling around Yorkshire's cricket clubs, *All Wickets Great and Small*, and there's no reason to break that momentum here either.

According to the map, it was a short walk to Peasholm Park, so Mrs Fuller could be introduced to the stellar entertainment that is the Battle of the River Plate re-enacted with model boats and booming guns.

With some of the practicalities out of the way, thoughts turned to the fixture list and interpreting it. The news was that Scarborough Cricket Club would welcome Surrey and

Worcestershire, inked in for June 25 and August 19 respectively to face Yorkshire in County Championship matches.

It struck me that the June encounter was arguably the higher-profile of the two with Surrey having signed Australian international all-rounder Mitchell Marsh to play all formats and boasting a squad stuffed with internationals.

Those at the Scarborough Cricket Festival in 2017 had witnessed world-class fast bowling from Essex's Mohammad Amir, whose career-best match figures of 10-72 sent Yorkshire crashing to defeat by eight wickets inside two days.

For that game, I had travelled over from Leeds on the train and spent the second day of the Festival on the coast. As fans passed through the gates, the weather was flawless and optimism coursed around the ground with that tell-tale, low-level hum of conversation.

Hours later, there were ashen faces as an embarrassing Yorkshire defeat became inevitable. When not wincing at the binary nature of Yorkshire's scorecard or staring incredulously at my watch; aghast at the way this match was progressing at breakneck speed, the magic of Scarborough was undiminished.

For 2018, Scarborough Cricket Club could be pleased at how their offering had expanded to 14 days of cricket overall, including two County Championship matches. For now, all that could wait. We now had our base booked; a mere nine months before the umpires would call 'play' for the first ball to be bowled.

January reconnaissance

It's 7 o'clock on a dark, late-January morning, but the railway station platform is filling, commuters into Leeds lining up like desolate penguins in suits and beanie hats.

There is a gnarly wind, prompting silent thanks at the choice of giant puffer coat that doubles my bulk and can feel like wrestling a duvet when trying to condense it down inside a train carriage.

Rocking back and forth to offset the nagging cold, hands crunched deep into pockets, thoughts turn to the day ahead in Scarborough. There's a meeting planned with Bill Mustoe (who stepped down as Chairman after 15 years in 2017) and committee member Rob Richtering, who I've got to know well from league cricket.

This will be a chance to hear their recollections, see the North Marine Road cricket ground out of season and walk the town to get a sense of the place beyond the usual regimented journey that fans make from the centre towards the clifftop like a line of ants.

There's a brief flash of panic in the drafty cathedral of Leeds railway station as the minutes tick by and I stand, alone, on the usual spot for any Scarborough train I've ever taken. Not a soul. Imagine tumbleweed cartwheeling across a dusty thoroughfare in a Western movie.

Opposite is the scrummage that is platform 17; the line from Liverpool to Hull that's rarely anything but a wall of humans – and one such DNA-packed scrum is watching a puzzled bloke gradually let the penny drop.

In fairness, I pass it off with effortless grace; pretending that I had always intended to take a lonely walk to peruse the monitors before sprinting up the stairs, three at a time, like a skinny rocket that's just been ignited.

The journey to Scarborough is a tranquil antidote; an advert for how rail travel can be effortless and stress-free when the stars align. For reasons I can't quite fathom, no-one is going to the coast – or at least not in any great number – so I have a table of four to myself.

The sun announces itself by yawning, stretching and then flooding the fields with golden light. Between York and Malton, a steep field on the left reveals a fence where, on either side, rows of sheep have gathered in horizontal lines like the countryside has been guerilla knitted overnight.

As we push past Malton, the vista opens and white picket fences punctuate the land, laid out for horse jumps. In the blink of an eye, it's as if we've time travelled to the land of Lilliput; in this expanse, the impromptu equine gym appears miniscule. A ram with a knotted coat sits and stares balefully at a feeding station.

Electricity transmission towers with their three sets of arms straddle the emerald vista, conjuring scolding mothers or gun-toting cowboys. Towards Seamer, a phalanx of saplings pass by; each with a companion wooden support post that catches the light like white crosses in a cemetery.

After a scenic hour, we arrive in Scarborough. The shackles come off when walking a town, not having the faintest clue where you're going. Upon arrival, with time to burn and nowhere to be, I gravitated to the downhill slope of Westborough; a main pedestrian artery through Scarborough down to South Bay and the harbour.

Above a shoe shop on the corner of Bar Street, there's a blue heritage plaque revealing that 'William 'Strata' Smith lived here.' Smith published the first geological map of England and Wales in 1815 and was a pioneer in the understanding of rock formation.

While having no particular passion for the investigation of rock through the layers of fossils, it served to demonstrate that you just never know what you'll find. If awarded the time to amble, I spend much of the time in a town or city looking up, to the curiosity of those barrelling by.

Off King Street, I spied tantalising reflections of the North Sea as dancing jewels of light and wound my way round to enjoy the abundant curvature of the beach. I found myself at the top of St Nicholas Gardens; terraced greenery next to the back of the Town Hall, a distinguished, red-brick, Grade II-listed building that encouraged me to stop and gawp.

There is something magical about catching sight of the sea for the first time. It instantly calms me. I feel the shackles fall away and it's possible to take a longer, deeper breath.

Doubling back, a prominent arrow-shaped sign above a sandwich bar nudged me to the prospect of the market on the next left and it was the smartest hunch I took all day. The cobbles of St Helen's Square had barely begun before the imposing hulk of Scarborough Market Hall revealed itself.

In through a giant blue door with gold floral inlaid panels, I paused to take in the scale of this proud architectural statement of Whitby stone that first opened in 1853. My visit felt well timed as there was a £2.8m refurbishment unveiled in 2017 and the resulting modern, vibrant space is a roaring success.

The main hall was very quiet, with the ground floor dominated by an explosion of colour from fruit and veg stalls. My first impressions were that the height of the roof gave it the feel of a gallery and everything was absolutely spick and span.

The crisp, dark grey signage on the individual units on the mezzanine level drew the eye and I wound my way up the circular staircase to investigate. From this vantage point, the family butcher M. Nockels was engrossed in the till by the entrance and traders were in conversation with each other while a few punters cradled a brew and passed the time.

Scarborough Radio was one of the occupied booths; a bloke in headphones by the window scanned a panel of buttons and flashing lights, though the 'On Air' sign wasn't lit. He was engrossed and didn't seem to notice as I gawped outside until the moment of voyeurism passed and I got to The Seafood Social cafe.

This is a social enterprise set up by Laura Whittle, the director of Whitby Seafoods, with all profits going to the Rainbow Centre, a charity that supports the homeless in the town and campaigns around related issues. Two of those interconnected strands are long-term unemployment and the effects of low wages, with Scarborough named as having the lowest mean pay in Britain by a thinktank, the Social Market Foundation.

That research is now several years old, but things don't change overnight and the high proportion of self-employment and seasonal work for Scarborians will continue to have an impact. I noticed that The Seafood Social has a 'Pay it Forward' scheme, where you can pay extra towards a scampi and chips or a brew, which then goes directly to those who desperately need support.

As I sat looking out towards Scarborough Castle and slurped on a Yorkshire Gold tea, it struck me that this was astute on-the-ground, community engagement (corporates call it 'social responsibility') that could be easily traced from concept to delivery.

By offering wages and training to those who have been unable to get work because of homelessness, poverty, a criminal record or substance misuse, the cafe raises vital funds, but also achieves its own mission statement.

Hands now well warmed, it was time to get back outside and have them instantly frozen again. A dapper shop frontage in baby blue, complete with banana yellow trim, piqued my interest around the corner. Bjorn Clogs has been making clogs by hand in Scarborough since 1978; not something I thought I'd ever write in these pages.

I had to hurry on to my meeting at Scarborough Cricket Club, so didn't have time to delve into the world of classic Swedish-style orthopaedic clogs with a wooden sole footbed, but the entrepreneurial drive in these parts is very much alive and kicking.

* * *

The start of North Marine Road is the final segment of a cricket fan's walk up to Yorkshire County Cricket Club's outground and, for the uninitiated, the tatty buildings don't exactly ratchet up the sense of sporting occasion.

Of course, this only amplifies the awe, once you dip left through gates and see the terrific grassy amphitheatre, cradled by wooden bench seating, but the final few minutes on foot from the chippy by the roundabout are underwhelming.

Scarborough Cricket Club is one of the jewels of this town and the plain and tired road sign above a newsagent doesn't reflect the regard in which it's held. There should really be something loud and proud shouting out 'County Cricket This Way!' though 'cricket ground' does appear (alongside the YMCA Leisure Centre) on a black signpost back in the centre.

The stretch of hotels and B&Bs that cater for the tourists during peak season looks a tad forlorn, with little sign of life, or maybe it's just that I've lost my joie de vivre as a ferocious wind rattles my eyes in their sockets, causing them to water like a leaky tap.

A sign outside the cricket club beckons me in with the news that the tea room is open; an off-season experiment designed to encourage the locals in to try a venue on their doorstep. On the left before the gates is the weathered, sandy-coloured brick wall with a Scarborough Cricket Club sign – 'Home to Scarborough cricket since 1863' emblazoned on a photo of a packed crowd.

Scarborough Cricket Club's emblem stands out; a set of stumps with crossed cricket bats positioned above the round motif of the 13th-century 'Common Seal of the Borough' depicting the castle and the harbour.

I spot the old turnstiles, not in use today. They're a work of art in themselves. Their wear and tear speaks to a life of ushering sports fans into North Marine Road. How many have squeezed through the waist-high barriers down the years?

In bold lettering, its purpose and maker dominate the brass top plate, cold to the touch, now aged with a mossy green patina. This 'Rush Preventative' example was crafted by W.T. Ellison & Co. Limited, Irlams o' th' Height, Manchester. From the 1890s, the company produced thousands for sports grounds, amusement parks and swimming pools.

Appropriately enough at the gateway to the Scarborough Cricket Festival, it acts as a portal; a reminder that you are about to step back in time.

I yank open the office door and hurl myself inside away from the howling wind to greet the Scarborough Cricket Club office team. Over a restorative brew, stories are teased out of Bill Mustoe, the Chairman here for 15 years, who stepped down from his post in 2017, but is very much still involved.

The conversation works its way around to the evolution of the North Marine Road pitches that have changed so markedly from how they used to be. After being asked about the slow and low nature of the Scarborough tracks in the Nineties, Fred Trueman was one such prevalent voice who suggested digging it all up and starting again.

Once the decision was taken, it was Mick Stewart (previously the groundsman at another Yorkshire County Cricket Club outpost, The Circle in Hull) who oversaw the process of digging down by between five and eight inches in a cricket version of *Time Team*.

The significant investment paid off and whether it was the Ongar Loam wedded to reconfigure the soil composition or advances in groundsmanship techniques, the end result was the birth of 'Scarbados' – a self-deprecating nod to North Yorkshire's version of Barbados and, in a cricket context, to the terrifyingly rapid West Indies wickets of old.

Ironically, in 2003, as Scarborough Cricket Club reinvented itself as a welcome coastal haven for fast bowlers, the Barbados pitch was being criticised by none other than 'Whispering Death' himself (Michael Holding) after West Indies quicks Tino Best and Jermaine Lawson had gone for 230 against Australia.

It got me thinking about the etymology of the word 'Scarbados' and whoever introduced it into the vernacular. It wasn't born out of the cricket, but as a witty response to criticism of the town's tourism. Barbados is derived from Portuguese or Spanish and translates as 'the bearded ones' – believed to be in reference to the panoply of bearded fig trees on the island.

A rudimentary dissection of Scarborough shows its meaning as the fortress (from Old Norse word 'borg') of Skarthi ('Hare-Lip') who was a Viking that formed a settlement in 966. So, when you think about it, Scarbados is really just a beard convention (translation: the 'hairy-lipped ones').

Viking-related wordplay aside, attention turns to the showbiz news of the week. Singer Britney Spears had confirmed she would be belting out a few tunes at the somewhat unlikely venue of Scarborough Open Air Theatre in August.

As luck would have it, she would be able to navigate the town's heritage and dip her toes in the frothing surf on the Saturday and then come to the cricket on the Sunday. I had tweeted her to remind her that Worcestershire were the visitors and have yet to hear back.

The fixture list for 2018 offered a glimpse of what the future could hold for Scarborough Cricket Club. Aside from county games, the England Under-19 Test and one-day international were inked for July against South Africa, as well as a Kia Super League fixture between Yorkshire Diamonds and Western Storm.

You always want these occasions to show off the best of the host cricket ground and I recall watching online as England Women took on India at Scarborough back in 2014; the first one-day international was a rain-affected affair with a tiny crowd.

That being said, it illustrated that the technology was present and correct to broadcast live cricket, with the England & Wales Cricket Board live streaming the match on YouTube. The ground misses out because access is a problem for the Sky Sports juggernaut of cabling and equipment at Scarborough. However, the fact the ECB's highlights package from that match has been viewed over a million times shows audiences can be reached without the media giants.

In some respects, it was fortunate that North Marine Road also had the next match as Charlotte Edwards' ninth ODI hundred helped England to a 2-0 series win, though I imagine it's difficult to fill grounds that hold successive games close together.

* * *

If I nudge you back to the present, as Bill Mustoe's yarns gather momentum, the evolution of the club continues as a theme. There's a frank discussion over journalist David Hopps' criticism of the ground a decade back and the club's subsequent effort to regenerate.

Some of you will remember the furore when a critical article appeared in *The Guardian* in 2009 where Hopps labelled the cricket ground as being in 'terminal decline' with a broken toilet, overflowing drain and evidence of swirling litter among the grievances lending it, in his words, a sense of squalor. For Hopps, the pointed message in print was borne from an anger and worry that the affection for Scarborough would only stretch so far and its future could be jeopardised, if left to fall into disrepair.

When I spoke with Hopps, he admitted to being pleased by the effect it caused: 'There are very few times in 40 years of journalism, where I think I've had such an obvious beneficial effect and that makes me happy because Scarborough is one of my three favourite grounds in the world.'

Having not been to North Marine Road for a few years, it was a collection of circumstances that precipitated the article Hopps wrote. Together, they sound like a sequence of mishaps from a Fawlty Towers episode.

First, dirty water from a blocked drainpipe at the back of the pavilion soaked his trousers. Next, the press room toilet wouldn't flush and the handle fell off. The ground was a mess, in his words. When he went to sit in the Popular Bank during the morning session, the seat was broken and so the frustration grew.

He thinks that the rose-tinted fondness for Scarborough blinded many: 'I am a big believer that people loved Scarborough so much, they were refusing to see the flaws, they were seeing their memories, they weren't actually seeing the truth of what the ground became.'

At the time, it was convenient to cast him as a villain,

but from our conversation Hopps felt that Scarborough Cricket Club, despite the efforts and loyalty of many, had been in danger of fading away. Nonetheless, the critical article provoked a fierce reaction and on the evening of the second day of the Festival, he got both barrels.

Former Yorkshire and England off-spinner Geoff Cope was outside the ground with his guide dog and a colleague pointed out Hopps across the road. Cue a bizarre shouting match with cars and buses providing the proverbial garden fence. As Hopps recalls with a chuckle, it went a little like this.

'It's an absolute disgrace what you wrote!'

'I'll come and see you tomorrow, Copey!'

'I won't want to talk to you!'

BBC Look North dispatched a camera crew to Scarborough to get the views of cricket fans, including one whose opinion on the broken seats was: 'I don't need a sofa to sit on!' which rather typified an acceptance of degradation.

While the club might have felt that the negative article was over the top, it is an example of cricket journalism precipitating change. It ultimately led to investment in North Marine Road and significant improvements. Scarborough Cricket Club bestowed on Hopps the honour of having the newly renovated press box toilet named after him. Hopps laughs it off as some way from the glory of a plaque, though he does intend to sponsor 'The Hopps Inn' at some point.

It comes with the job as a journalist to expect forthright

responses to articles, particularly on the sacrament of Yorkshire cricket, and David recalls an epic telling-off that lasted the mile or so walk towards North Marine Road. 'Yorkshire and England wicketkeeper-batsman, David Bairstow, once gave me a rollicking that started roughly at the Palm Court Hotel and went all the way to the ground. He didn't pause for breath for about 25 minutes! That makes me smile when I remember it.'

According to Bill Mustoe, the written barbs in the national press did sting, but they also prompted action once the money had been sourced. But that may never have happened, had it not been for a polite enquiry from someone using a wheelchair.

A Scarborough member, Mrs Grace, asked Bill one day about wheelchair accessibility to the pavilion and he arranged for a ramp to be fitted. In a subsequent conversation, she thanked him and casually mentioned that her son worked for the supermarket Tesco. In his capacity as Chairman sniffing out a commercial opportunity, Bill pondered to himself what Mr Grace's job might be for the retailer.

It turned out Kevin Grace was a director for the supermarket giant and that chance meeting with his mother ultimately led to Tesco choosing Scarborough Cricket Club as its Community Partner with a £3m investment transforming swathes of the ground.

The pavilion was a chief beneficiary with a new cellar, lift installation and bar, with complete refurbishment, decoration, fixtures and fittings. From concrete to cosmetic, major upgrades also included an overhaul of the Tea Room, complete with a balcony area, new bench seating on the Popular Bank, while toilets and scoreboards were rehabilitated. Not to forget 'The Hopps Inn' sign as a nod to the spark of motivation and a dash of humour to show there were no hard feelings.

Around the same time, Scarborough Cricket Club also engaged with NatWest CricketForce, a national initiative to help cricket clubs improve their facilities through volunteers donating a weekend for pre-season repairs. Some 350 people turned up to volunteer in March 2010, galvanised in part by the negative headlines about the town and the cricket club.

As Mike Gatting, from the England and Wales Cricket Board, and former Yorkshire captain, David Byas, put a lick of paint on the West Stand railings and the outfield was filled with children, Mustoe could be heartened by the response.

At the time, he likened keeping the county ground in shape akin to painting the Forth Rail Bridge in Scotland; once a perpetual task that began again as soon as it ended. Though let's hope Scarborough's fortunes are less dramatic than maintaining the rusting rivets and creaking 23,000 miles of cable over the Firth of Forth.

The community volunteering effort had been engineered by Geoff Cope in his capacity as a trustee and a partnership was forged with Yorkshire Coast College so students could get hands-on experience at a sports stadium. Of course, the real challenge is maintaining that momentum year-after-year and that continual enthusiasm is just as tough for Scarborough as it is for a little village club.

* * *

Part of the many strands to writing this book was to talk to and meet those for whom county cricket at Scarborough has become a ritual over the years. I heard about a group of London doctors who would visit the Festival and spectate, drink and act as medical assistance, should they be needed. In what order those three things took place I can well imagine. You wouldn't want to get the kiss of life in the evening session, let's put it that way.

Speaking of illness and injury, Bill recalled the time the umpire Trevor Jesty had to leave the field for about an hour, due to illness, in Yorkshire's Festival game against Sussex in 2011.

Yorkshire's first-team coach Craig White deputised for a while, but then handed the reins over to local league umpire Fred Bernard who was more used to duty in the Scarborough Beckett Cricket League. Bernard, 75 years young and watching the action from the stands, was approached by the Scarborough umpires' secretary from the hospitality tent and as someone who had yet to sink a few pints, duly won a swift promotion.

Rules governing the involvement of non-first-class cricket officials meant that Fred could only cast his beady eye from square leg on run outs and stumpings rather than taking up the usual position for an umpire at the bowler's end. It sounded as if he had a blast, but, perhaps to his relief, the next 55 minutes passed without incident.

Though making his first-class umpiring debut, Bernard was not entirely green when it came to Yorkshire matches, having officiated three times before in benefit and friendly matches. But, as Yorkshire lost 5-63 in 22 overs for a productive session, this was definitely one for his scrapbook.

Now, Dickie Bird is someone for whom everyone in Yorkshire has a story. Dickie had forgotten his suit for a cricket function on one occasion, nipped into a Scarborough charity shop and picked up a bargain piece of haute couture.

Mustoe doesn't recall saying it, but when asked by Dickie how he looked, is said to have replied: 'Dickie, you look like a thousand lira!' Those conversant with pre-Euro Italian currency will appreciate the tongue-in-cheek remark, as spiking inflation rendered Italy's high-denomination banknotes as prized as Monopoly money.

Another of Bill's tales that made me chuckle was when Scarborough Cricket Club Secretary, Colin Adamson, was sent out to quieten a rebellion caused by Geoffrey Boycott's non-selection.

In 1981, Yorkshire's Team Manager Ray Illingworth dropped Geoffrey Boycott on the morning of the three-day match against Northamptonshire. Unhappy supporters gathered in front of the pavilion with the usual start of play at 11am approaching. So, Colin was dispatched to, well, I've no idea what the plan was and neither did he, maybe shoo them away.

But, Boycott was not picked and that was that, so fans gradually returned to their seats of their own accord. Protests are not uncommon in the realm of Yorkshire County Cricket Club, just not usually at the expense of the cricket itself.

Boycott's replacement that day was Yorkshire's current Director of Cricket Martyn Moxon, drafted in for one of his earliest – and most unforgettable – games at Scarborough. He was staying with team-mate Simon Dennis and had to hotfoot it to North Marine Road, after getting a call on Simon's home phone at 9 o'clock that morning.

'I got to the ground and it was a weird atmosphere. I remember going out to bat with Richard Lumb. This guy came up to me, into my face, and said, "We haven't come to watch you, you know!" There were a number of spectators sat on the outfield for a period of time and we couldn't start the game.'

While Colin wasn't required for crowd dispersal that day, it does suggest that for all of Scarborough's geniality, it has not been immune from the drama that swirls around Yorkshire County Cricket Club.

* * *

As Bill Mustoe takes his leave, we head over to the tea room; that West-facing bungalow with 'TEA ROOM' painted in bold, white lettering on its angled roof as a navigational prompt to the skies for other life forms seeking to quench their thirst.

As those who read my regular cricket musings will know all too well, cricket teas feature prominently in my priorities on any given day. At Scarborough Cricket Club, the tea room is a popular feature with uninterrupted views of the cricket and the pavilion.

Colin reckoned that there has been one in that present location since 1888; an acknowledgement that cricket alongside the infusion of tea leaves has long since had its merit in these parts. In more recent times (the last decade), a decision was made to change the all-important menu, switching to everything being home-made and Scarborough Cricket Club saw their sales rocket.

Today, I'm content to slurp on a soup, dunk handfuls of bread roll and gaze out of the window to watch a flock of gulls congregate on the grass just off the square; in that moment, they're parked where a fast bowler would run up, as if respectfully observing the sanctity of the playing area.

After a restorative bite, we seek solace back in the club offices and it's there that a chance comment by committee member Rob Richtering leads to a discussion on illegal betting; not something you imagine is rife in this seaside town.

On the noticeboard in the foyer is an 'anti-courtsider provision notice' from Yorkshire County Cricket Club and within its written warnings lies a glimpse into the darker side of illegal betting. With the eruption of betting online has come specific challenges for county cricket grounds around the use of phones and laptops or tablets on match days.

If there's suitable lag in broadband connectivity and they're quick enough, there's nothing to stop someone at a Festival match placing an illegal bet based on an action, such as a no-ball, wicket or six, that has already literally just happened. We're talking fractions of a second here and while televised matches might be deemed to hold a greater risk, there's a watchful eye for any untoward behaviour that officials are alerted to.

Anyone suspected of such activities can be ejected from the ground and banned for life, but identifying this behaviour must be specialist work given how many of us are glued to our phones or wear headphones to listen to radio commentary.

* * *

With such nefarious exploits ringing in my ears, I bid farewell and wind my way down from the ground in a south-easterly direction along Eastborough to the South Bay harbour, past handbags, body piercing, fudge, a tattoo parlour and a joke shop. I try not to mentally edit the grammar of the signage, but it's a well-worn habit. My internal monologue is debating the use of hyphenation in a do-nut when the sight of the sea elicits a smile.

Down here, cricket is a world away with the twinkling bulbs of amusement arcades jostling for attention on one side of Foreshore Road, with the serious business of the

RNLI Scarborough lifeboat station on West Pier across the way. It's one of the oldest still in use, founded in 1801 and first launched into service on November 2 that year when a crew of seven was rescued from the *Aurora* of Newcastle.

The work of the Royal National Lifeboat Institution, as the charity that saves lives at sea around our island's shores, really is something. I will never forget watching one of their boats bobbing out of Bridlington harbour at night in spiteful, raging seas like a brave champagne cork on a mission.

The tide is in, so there's not far to tread to get onto the sands and approach the gurgling, foaming waters of the North Sea that mimics the to and fro of the coin pusher in arcades; that seaside tourism staple nudging coins tantalisingly back and forth.

My route had come full circle, by chance, given the absence of a concrete plan, as there was nowhere obvious to park myself, reflect and defrost with a tea. So, I picked my way up the steep steps of St Nicholas Gardens with its neat, angular greenery and took a moment to catch my breath at the top as Queen Victoria watched from her plinth.

One of only seven original bronze statues of the Queen by sculptor Charles Bell Birch, she stands with the folds of her gown spilling over the edge of the plinth, holding those symbols of monarchy, the orb and sceptre. Today, against the painter's canvas of a bold sky, she looks a little tired; though I pause in her company long enough to discount heading inside the Grand Hotel in search of sustenance.

When it was completed in 1867, this 'immense structure

in red brick with tawny terracotta dressings,' (as Historic England puts it) was the largest hotel in Europe and must have been quite the lavish statement.

In 1887, it acknowledged that the popularity of the Scarborough Cricket Festival could help secure its status as the top hotel in the town, so the dining room was made available to cricket fans.

A proper visit would wait for another time, but it dominates as the eye sweeps the curve of South Bay with the red carriages of the Central Tramway alongside; a convenient traverse to the beach from Marine Parade up top for those partial to a funicular railway.

For now, I also discounted another hotel with links to Scarborough cricket; the Royal Hotel once had Hughie's Bar, of which I'd heard so much in relation to raucous nights after a day of county cricket. I asked for a cafe recommendation in the Town Hall and the glowing report of Greensmith & Thackwray turned out to be well judged.

The black sign with its bold golden lettering nods to the shop's past role as an 'Indian and colonial outfitters.' A delve into the archives reveals its retail history stretches back to the 1850s as a shop with clientele from nobility and high society.

Back in the late 1870s, the shop advertised 'under clothing of every kind', but a century or so later, it was coming to the end of its life. Online, I discovered a vintage retro dark green cricket tie by Greensmith & Thackwray from the 1980s, just before it closed its doors.

Now reinvented as a coffee shop, no longer sellers of

hosiery but of banana bread, a gentle hour was spent writing notes for this book and watching a couple's terrier strain at its leash to attempt to gulp down a ciabatta on a nearby table.

As a toasty refuge, it was one to note for future trips; not least because they do proper tea. You know it's a serious business when your teapot comes with an egg timer; with the aim to watch as seconds ebb away in granular form before the loose tea is ready to release its riches.

Walking the streets of Scarborough had been a way to break the ice; to connect with the town beyond its cricket club and appreciate that it has its own personality beyond chips on the benches while watching cover drives and stumps go cartwheeling.

Festival heyday:
The 6th Test

Originally, when mapping out this book, I decided not to linger on the Festival from past centuries or to achieve a forensic re-telling of bygone years. Yet, to ignore the way that the Scarborough Cricket Festival was born and evolved would be to do it and you a disservice.

Besides, while some of you will be avid Yorkshire County Cricket Club historians who know your Hawke from your Hutton, others won't have that interest or knowledge to call upon. So, you may not know that the Festival used to be a grander occasion that lasted for several weeks with the best of the best featuring.

In fact, cricket was played at Scarborough before the advent of the Festival, with one particular game catching my eye, when Scarborough Cricket Club played a team of Australian Aborigines over three days. It took place from August 27-29, 1869, at Castle Hill Yard and the aborigines won by 10 wickets. The scorecard was annotated with a player's name and the colour of their cap to distinguish between Aboriginal Australians, so it would say 'Mosquito – magenta.'

It all started in 1875, when Lord Londesborough put his hand in his pocket to sponsor a match between the Marylebone Cricket Club (MCC) and Yorkshire. It was to be a crucial patronage that would put Scarborough prominently on the map when it came to cricket. The MCC team was assembled by C.I. (Charles Inglis) Thornton who was an MCC member and also knew of Scarborough from frequent trips. Thus began a prominent annual fixture around which the Festival grew.

A year later, the planets perfectly aligned for the creation of a cricket event that continues today over a century and a half later (the interruption of the war years were the only break). Lord Londesborough became MCC President and cricket at Scarborough was enhanced to nine days. The headline fixture was once more MCC vs Yorkshire, with C.I. Thornton overseeing the MCC side.

This first Scarborough Cricket Festival in 1876 was played on a different site to the modern HQ of North Marine Road. Castle Hill in Scarborough hosted the inaugural Festival fixture where W.H. Hadow scored 126 out of 294 and Yorkshire were soundly beaten by mustering only 46.

While the prestigious attendance of the MCC was as regular as clockwork for nearly 100 years, part of what has symbolised the allure of Scarborough has been the variety of games. Gentlemen (amateurs) vs Players (professionals) was a popular fixture with team loyalties divided across England's class system.

In 1963, the MCC abolished the notion of amateurism

when all first-class cricketers became professional. It sparked a turning point in the Scarborough Cricket Festival calendar as the game that had been played since 1875 was suddenly no more, though the advent of sponsored matches was around the corner.

A recurring theme from the conversations I've had is how the Scarborough Cricket Festival, while magnificent, is not what it once was. For those that currently revel in four days of County Championship duelling, that might seem a little curmudgeonly.

Yet, for many decades, Scarborough was the pitstop that signalled the end of the county season and touring countries would bookend their stay in England, after the international cricket, with a match at North Marine Road.

So many famous names have graced the Scarborough Cricket Festival and chief among them was Australian batsman Don Bradman who scored 153 in his last-ever innings in England. The tourists earned the nickname 'The Invincibles' for being the first international side to remain unbeaten in every game on a tour to England.

On September 10-13, 1948, Australia came back to Yorkshire for the third time on an arduous tour where the Scarborough Cricket Festival would be the 32nd match of a groaning schedule that had started on April 30.

Bradman's last hurrah was the talking point as H.D.G. Leveson-Gower's XI managed to draw with the Australians after the tourists' first innings closed on 489. After the game, Yorkshire County Cricket Club awarded honorary life membership to Bradman, with the Australian accepting a silver tray.

The Australians had been coming to North Marine Road since the three-day game in September 1878 against the Gentlemen of England that ended in a draw. The last time the Aussies were at Scarborough was when they took on Yorkshire in 1977. The three-day match that July was also a draw with Boycott's 103 in the second innings helping Yorkshire to 233-5 after being shot out for 75 first up.

Thereafter, until 1995, the Scarborough Cricket Festival regularly hosted the tourists whether it was T.N. Pearce's XI taking on New Zealand (1978), D.B. Close XI against Sri Lanka (1984) or the World XI facing Pakistan (1992).

It was the West Indies of 1995 who were the last full international men's side to appear at Scarborough (with a nod to England Lions vs Sri Lanka A in 2011).

The record will show that the scorecard read: West Indians (426 & 356-4 declared) drew with Yorkshire (297 & 143-3). However, someone wasn't reading from the script. The crowd berated the West Indies for not choosing to stop their innings earlier on the final day to give the hosts a sporting chance of victory.

Nonetheless, there were centuries by five separate batsmen, a five-wicket haul in an otherwise chastening few days to be a bowler and Keith Arthurton hit what some still talk about as the largest six they've ever seen.

Mark Robinson, now England's women's coach, could only watch as Arthurton crunched him for a mighty maximum that left the ground like a shooting star. Surely the winner of the £100 jackpot on offer for the largest six of the Festival that year?

Someone who remembers it well is Ian Philliskirk, who has notched over 10,000 runs in the Bradford League for the likes of Baildon, Farsley and Lightcliffe.

He was brought up two streets down from the cricket ground in Scarborough after moving to the town as a nine-year-old. Summers were spent watching as much cricket as possible and a young Philliskirk would operate the scoreboard alongside scorer Tony Jack.

Ian recalls one gargantuan blow that went up and up: 'The legend had it that Carl Hooper hit one into the sea in 1991, but that's not been verified! I remember Arthurton coming in and teeing off in 1995. We were sat in the West Stand and he hit the roof of the Trafalgar Stand end hotels, which is a massive hit.'

Philliskirk can also picture Chris Cairns getting hold of Richard Stemp (figuratively) and belting a series of whopping maximums that hit the wall, but it was Arthurton that was the furthest strike he saw at North Marine Road. When it comes to big hitters, everyone you talk to has a story. Their eyes light up, eyebrows wrinkle in concentration as individual feats are excavated from the memory bank.

It takes a monumental blow to hit a cricket ball clear out of Scarborough's ground, but particularly so to clear the houses and reach Trafalgar Square. The club thinks it has been done on three occasions. If you believe Lord Hawke's biography, C.I. Thornton in 1875 is said to have hit a six that struck a roof of one of the houses outside of the ground. Maybe he did it twice, as J.M. Kilburn records that Thornton's knock in 1886 of 107 in little over an hour included one that went clear into Trafalgar Square.

Gervais Frederic Wells-Cole was a right-handed batsman from Brigg in Lincolnshire who made a guest appearance for Scarborough in 1901 against the Gentlemen of Yorkshire. I couldn't find any reference to this particular match in the official records, but he is said to have bludgeoned 387. Its absence from official data suggests it might have been a more casual match, though the opposition was anything but, and a triple hundred surely deserves its place in history.

Last but by no means least is Cec Pepper who was part of the Australian Services XI that played a H.D.G. Leveson-Gower side in September 1945. He is said to have been offered a bet by wicketkeeper Arthur Wood to try to clear the houses.

Well, he did just that; the first to do so in a century and he had a match to remember as his 168 off 148 balls was a satisfying landmark; Pepper had never reached three figures in first-class cricket before.

Nowadays, in televised T20 cricket at any rate, there is an immediate calculation of the length of hits, though I wonder if wind speed and other ponderables like the flight path of an errant goose are factored in. There's an excellent article online by Charles Davis for *The Cricket Monthly* that delves into the notion of the longest six struck.

The obvious conundrum being that no-one is able to track the ball with mathematical precision from impact to destination, though Davis used Google Earth measurements to aid his shortlist. C.I. Thornton is referenced as a majestic six-hitter, whose efforts are meant to have easily surpassed modern maximums from powerful strikers such as Chris Gayle, but we can't know if that was where it landed or where it rolled and finished up.

* * *

For a cricket club that needed to be dragged kicking and screaming into the age of overseas players, beginning with Sachin Tendulkar in 1992, Yorkshire have recruited some masterful exponents of bat and ball since to make up for lost time.

If you were to take a scalpel to the smorgasbord of statistics and individual batting feats that span the years at Scarborough, Jacques Rudolph would feature prominently.

Wherever he played, the South African was simply prolific for Yorkshire from 2007 to 2011 in a purple patch that yielded 5,429 first-class runs at an average of 52. At North Marine Road, he was unstoppable.

In limited-overs cricket, Scarborough became a second home and Rudolph concluded his county career having averaged 99 on the ground. It was a rate of productivity that rivalled the former international batsman's efforts anywhere else in the world.

Nowadays, Rudolph has his own travel company and we caught up by phone to test Jacques' memory and rekindle the good old days. Unsurprisingly, Scarborough makes his top three favourite cricket grounds:

'What I enjoyed about it was that it has quite a quaint-little-club feel, but of all the grounds I've played on in the world, it's probably my best record. It was a brilliant pitch. Playing at Scarborough was definitely one of the highlights of my career.'

When he was signed for Yorkshire, Rudolph came as a 'Kolpak' player, meaning he wasn't technically classed as an overseas cricketer. The Kolpak exemption was named after the Slovak handball player who won a court ruling that stated those from countries with a European Union Association Agreement could have the same freedom to travel and work as EU citizens.

It was one of the most significant controversies for English domestic cricket in the last 50 years, which really is saying something. For a county of Yorkshire's creed favouring home-grown cricketers over foreign imports, Rudolph's arrival sharply split opinion.

Of course, Jacques hadn't taken the decision lightly. He had forfeited the right to play for his country to ensure qualification, but there was still a sense that the Yorkshire cricketing public were waiting to see if all the fuss had been worth it. Acceptance came by virtue of sheer weight of runs. Yorkshire fans might grumble about you not being from Hull or Harrogate, but they will also respect someone who scores hundreds again and again.

For Jacques, the Clydesdale Bank 40 semi-final against Warwickshire in September 2010 was a special moment. As he left the field having scored 106, there was raucous appreciation:

'The one thing I vividly remember was walking off the field to a standing ovation, which turned out to be one of my last games at Scarborough. Speaking about it now, it still gives me goosebumps.'

The allure of Scarborough wasn't just because Rudolph felt confident walking out to bat there. Representing South Africa took him to large international stadiums and North Marine Road was a world away from that:

'Especially playing Test cricket and playing at big grounds, it doesn't have the same charisma of a smaller field. I can think of other places like Arundel and Cheltenham, those kind of fields I used to adore.'

In that four-and-a-half-year adventure with Yorkshire, Jacques has quite the scrapbook to call upon, including playing in the 2011 match where Joe Root scored his first century in first-class cricket (160 against Sussex).

Rudolph also got to know the Bairstow family well during his time in the county, particularly Janet, the mum of Yorkshire and England batsman Jonny Bairstow. Jacques was obviously a long way from home and family so found comfort in spending time at the Bairstow home for dinners or popping over for a brew.

'I was very close with his mother. She was like my Yorkshire mother! At the time, my wife was studying to be a doctor in South Africa, so I was by myself quite a lot. We just used to get on really well.'

Had Rudolph stayed another year in county cricket, he could even have qualified for England, but those five years at Yorkshire County Cricket Club had matured his game and ultimately helped propel him back into the South African national side. A return to county cricket with Glamorgan was Rudolph's swansong, but wearing the White Rose has stayed with him:

'If I'm brutally honest with you, my dream was to finish my career at Yorkshire, but unfortunately it didn't pan out that way.'

* * *

It's not just the distance of the hits that stirs the crowd at Scarborough, as much as their frequency and the pedigree of the players who deliver the blows, or those who have to stand and watch, with indignation, as an attempted off-spinner or over-pitched yorker is jettisoned towards the ocean.

On a stark January afternoon, I picked up the phone to Rob Sproston, an agent with a roster of celebrities and sports stars on his books, who used to source the international cricketers for the World XI and other sides.

Talking to Rob beamed us back to a time when Scarborough was still the unofficial final 'Test' of the summer for whichever nation was touring England. In 1984, he began his involvement by recruiting a few names to play for the Brian Close XI against the Sri Lankans, many of whom were already in the UK as overseas professionals.

That year, Desmond Haynes hit 111 out of 308-5

declared for Brian Close's side with any slim chance of a result wrecked as the third day was washed out. Martyn Moxon did bag three wickets in a relatively rare appearance with the ball as Yorkshire tried seven bowling options.

The availability of the overseas stars is a principle reason why the Festival is seen as having diminished to being a shadow of its former self. Sproston's connections yielded the likes of Martin Crowe and Brian Lara to come to the North Yorkshire coast. It must have been a fun time to be an agent and Scarborough was the place to be, long before the proliferation of T20 tournaments.

The length of the Festival in the Eighties wasn't much longer than now, but rather than a four-day County Championship fixture, it was a three-day match, awarded first-class status, along with two one-day matches.

As he has mentioned in kindly penning a foreword for this book, Michael Parkinson had a stint as President of the Festival. In fact, Michael Parkinson's World XI weren't to be beaten with Dennis Lillee turning out with his right-arm rockets and Pakistan's Imran Khan leading the side in 1988.

Parkinson's brief tenure over superstars against the MCC (twice) and then India will be remembered fondly for a flowing hall of fame, with hundreds by Martin Crowe, Carlisle Best, Wayne Larkins, Mudassar Nasir, Sachin Tendulkar and two in the same match from Mark Greatbatch.

It speaks to a different time when famous cricketers from around the world were available because they were already in the country and there was less cricket played. It pre-dated the 20-over format and all of the T20 leagues across the world, from the Indian Premier League to the Pakistan Super League, along with the short-form fireworks here in the UK.

The more I researched Scarborough Cricket Festival matches, the more rabbit holes I happily fell down and we can divide them between those with first-class status and those without.

Between its incarnation in 1876 until the 2018 match against Worcestershire, there have been 255 first-class games involving Yorkshire at Scarborough (of course, not all of them were Festival games, but most were).

Amid those opponents such as the MCC, counties and touring international sides, were the odd surprise such as the Canadians who toured in 1954 and took on Yorkshire at Scarborough at the end of August. It was the last of their four first-class games and was scheduled as a three-day game but the Canadians lost by 249 runs with a day to spare.

If I'm honest, it has been the other games that have sparked my interest more. An unsettled programme in the Sixties for the Scarborough Cricket Festival led to a drop in the club's membership and as a new decade dawned, thoughts turned to how to tap into the popularity of limited-overs cricket instead.

The Fenner Trophy proved to be the canny solution and ran between 1971 and 1981. It boosted the club's coffers and was a seminal moment when a historic fixture was canned and a new dawn ushered in.

The engineering company J.H. Fenner & Co. Ltd of Hull sponsored this successful attempt to reinvigorate the Scarborough Cricket Festival and a decade of patronage followed. The competition always involved Yorkshire and the three other winners from the County Championship, the John Player League and the Gillette Cup.

To make space for this bold vision, Yorkshire and MCC agreed to cancel their traditional fixture and so it disappeared and never came back to Scarborough. If this was a shock to those brought up on a diet of three-day cricket, the cricket club's finances had never been rosier.

* * *

The format and volume of the Scarborough Cricket Festival was changing. A central figure at Yorkshire County Cricket Club in this transition period was Geoffrey Boycott, whose first-class career spanned 1962 to 1986.

He liked batting at Scarborough, playing there more often than anywhere else but Headingley, and accumulated over 4,000 first-class runs at North Marine Road. I spoke to Geoffrey one spring morning to test his memory and to cast his mind back to his first innings at Scarborough.

'It was the Wednesday before bank holiday in August, we were staying at the Salisbury Hotel. That year, I'd given up working for the Ministry of Pensions and National Insurance in Barnsley. I went to work as a civil servant for four to five years after leaving Hemsworth Grammar

School.'

As something of a distraction, I look up Boycott's school online to see if he features, and, lo and behold, there is a first-eleven photo from 1955 with the results – young Boycott having averaged 9.4 with the bat and 2.5 with the ball! It offers a note of congratulations to Boycott on his selection for the Yorkshire Schoolboys and observes that he received his Yorkshire cap in the match against Derbyshire.

Boycott chose his career with cricket in mind, as the civil service were one of the few employers who allowed him to take holidays in blocks of two or three days. The aim was to break his way into the Yorkshire Second team which played two-day matches. That duly happened and sometimes there was one or more two-day matches in a week. He had to serve his apprenticeship like everyone else.

'When I started to be included in the twelve for Yorkshire, I'd suddenly get a telegram asking me to go. I finished up being twelfth man (reserve) most of the time. I think it was the pretence that I was in the squad, but anyhow, it was a learning curve and I enjoyed running errands for the players, getting cigarettes and this and that.'

But Boycott was using up three days of holiday at a time and he finally got in the team consistently in 1963, with England call-ups requiring Yorkshire to select a few Colts (junior players). Geoffrey recalls playing in the three-day game against Warwickshire at Scarborough.

Through performances, he had forced his way into this

strong Yorkshire side, but was acutely aware that he needed to be consistent. Unbeknown to him, a change was afoot that would shape his career.

'Just after breakfast on the Wednesday morning, Brian Close the captain said: "I want you to go in first today." Whoah, I said, no thanks, I'm doing alright at five and six. I'd given up my job in the civil service because they promised me I could have time off without pay when my holidays ran out, but when it came to it, they denied it to me. So, I had to make a decision: do I leave the civil service with no job, no pay, no contract with Yorkshire, nothing? All I got was a match fee if I played.'

So, playing cricket for Yorkshire wasn't just the ambition, it was the only way to earn his keep. Boycott had taken the gamble of being able to make it in county cricket and he seemed to be forging his way. Now, Close wanted him promoted up the order and that represented a risk.

'I was keen to do well to stay in the team and earn some money, which I did, but I had no guarantee. The first team were only on yearly agreements, anyhow. So, he wanted me to go in first, but I wasn't keen on the new ball! I was doing alright. He said: "Well, you've got two choices. You can either go in first or be twelfth man." I said, "You can't do that to me!" He said, "I'm the captain, I can do what I want." That made my mind up pretty quick!'

Yorkshire batted first and were dismissed for 301 with G. Boycott making 62, then he mustered 28 second time around as the home side won by 92 runs and Boycott passed 1,000 County Championship runs for the season.

We don't always know what's best for us, do we? In Boycott's case, he became one of the most prolific opening batsmen for county and country and it all began at Scarborough.

We get to enthusing about the Scarborough wow factor and why the Yorkshire public love it: 'It's reminiscent of when we were kids. You went to Scarborough for your holidays. It was the magic of going to the seaside, going on the beach, paddling in the sea, making sandcastles and riding the donkeys.'

His parents would take young Boycott over by coach for the day, a spot of lunch when the sea came in, a visit to the amusement park before fish and chips late afternoon, then the bus set off back at 5.30 the 80 miles or so to the village of Fitzwilliam near Wakefield.

Boycott also remembers how popular the cricket was: 'Scarborough would be full. 12,000 people would fill the ground and so it had such a wonderful atmosphere.'

Geoffrey Boycott's relationship with Scarborough extends to how he wrapped up a career that yielded 48,426 first-class runs with a final hurrah on the ground. It was September 10, 1986, and the last match of the Britannic Assurance County Championship season.

There was to be no fairytale ending or glory up for grabs; instead a mid-table clash with nothing riding on it. Boycott scored 61 before being run out when an attempted second run was cut short from a deft pick-up-and-throw by Alan Walker at fine leg.

Jim Love was his batting partner and though he was

blamed in Boycott's autobiography, Geoffrey appeared in magnanimous mood when we spoke. Was it a mix-up?

'No, I was a dozy booger, wasn't I? My fault. Alan Walker had a brilliant arm and I'd forgotten about it.'

As it transpired, Boycott missed out on the chance to bat again – and score the eight runs for the 1,000 runs-in-a-season landmark – as Northamptonshire followed on but finally declared at 5.21pm after reaching 422-8. So, a low-key end to a magnificent career ended without pomp or ceremony as fans drifted away, uncertain if Yorkshire would get the chance to bat again in the embers of the match – which they didn't.

Boycott's running battles with Yorkshire's committee had convinced him that the knives were out, despite the members' revolution of 1984 when Peter Fretwell displaced Fred Trueman on Yorkshire's committee and Boycott was ultimately reinstated as a player.

'I didn't ask people to stand up for me, but they did. You can't hope they'd do that again. I just knew it was time to go. I knew deep down.' Even talking about it all these years later, there is a profound sadness in his voice.

He showered and packed up his bag for the last time, by which time the spectators and players had left: 'I just walked round the whole ground while people were cleaning up. I had a last walk round, a look at it, I knew that I'd let it come to an end.'

* * *

The chance to talk to Boycott's batting partner that day, Jim Love, who racked up 10,355 first-class runs for Yorkshire in 250 games, happened more by luck than judgement.

We had agreed to meet at Castleford Cricket Club for one of Yorkshire Under-19s midweek games, as he is now Yorkshire's Elite Junior Cricket Coordinator. I got my days mixed and turned up on completely the wrong day.

In a sign that Lady Luck was smiling, not only were Yorkshire Under-19s' playing another fixture at the same club on that day, but just as the penny was dropping that I had miscalculated, Jim turned up anyway, quite by chance.

Yorkshire were batting and into their second innings against Warwickshire as we sat outside on the seats of the pavilion and watched cricketers chase leather over the enormous oval at Savile Park.

Between us, we try to recall which one-day trophy his abiding memory of Scarborough relates to; it may be the Fenner Trophy Final of 1978 as it was against Northamptonshire. Love doesn't want to mention the culprit of the practical joke he's about to tell me – but that soon becomes apparent from the description.

'It was one of the funniest moments I can recall. We had an opening batter who had, how can I put it, a lack of hair. He was the smartest cricketer ever and the last thing he ever did was put his cap on when he went out to bat. This one day, unbeknown to him, someone had put itching powder in his cap.

'We all saw it done and didn't say anything and as he put it on, this cloud of itching powder all shot down his neck and onto his head. We were roaring with laughter as soon as he left the changing room. He got out halfway to the middle and the cap came off. He was scraping his head which went on for a few minutes. He got a first-baller and when he came back in, everybody had cleared the changing room. He wasn't a happy bunny.'

The other game involving Northamptonshire, and the one for which Love is most famous, is the Benson & Hedges Cup Final at Lord's in 1987 where his 75 not out won him the man-of-the-match award, back then named the Gold award. Love defended the last ball of the match to keep the scores level on 244, but Yorkshire won, by virtue of losing fewer wickets.

I've no idea what would have happened, had Love gone for a yahoo off the last ball and been bowled, as both teams would be on the same total and wickets down. Answers on a postcard.

Itchy antics on Boycott aside, we talk about the feisty nature of the crowds back then who, he reckons, barracked more than they do now.

The reason for that, Love believes, is that there was more social interaction between the players and supporters after the game sharing a pint in the bar. I guess fans got to know players better and felt more inclined to give a rollocking – although in my experience that's rarely been in short supply.

'I played once in sea fret at the Festival and I probably played one of my best innings. I don't think hardly anybody saw it! I think I got 70 or 80 and it was brilliant to bat in. It was just a white wall but because it wasn't a first-class game, we played on.'

One of the most extraordinary memories has to be when a plane passed over the cricket ground and crashed into the North Sea on the last day of the Schweppes County Championship fixture against Gloucestershire in 1983.

'We were fielding at the time and there was a huge Vulcan jet, or something like that, a bloody great big thing. We saw it climb and then there was a huge bang. Half the crowd dashed across to the other side of the road to see what had happened.'

It was a Royal Air Force Lightning plane that was travelling from RAF Binbrook to Teesside International airport to take part in an air show. The pilot, flight lieutenant Mike Thompson, was doing a fly-past for nearby RAF recruiting station Scalby Mills outside Scarborough when there was believed to be a mechanical failure.

In an act of supreme courage, Thompson chose not to eject to safety as that could well have meant the plane crashed on North Bay beach, packed with thousands of holidaymakers. Instead, he manoeuvred out to sea and sacrificed his own life.

Sat in Castleford watching Yorkshire age group cricket that day, neither of us knew the story to its fullest extent, but I steered the conversation around to Jim's top knock at Scarborough. He makes a passing reference to a hundred notched up there, but laughs at another near-miss:

'The knock I remember most is one delivery where I was lbw on 99. I joined the 99 club. It was just a misjudgement on my part. I wasn't really thinking about it too much. I was just going to work it for one, have done with it and I missed it. I had one of those where you look up at the umpire and think, "That's out, isn't it?" and he nods at you and you go. He didn't bother with the finger!'

As for tricky bowlers, a Roses tussle came to mind: 'I remember facing Wasim Akram for the first time. He played this Sunday League game there and I didn't really like wearing helmets. I was actually one of the first to wear one as a short-leg fielder. I got likened to Mrs Shilling and all sorts at Ascot. I could show you the bloody cuttings of that my mother kept.

'I always remember Warren Hegg saying, "You should have a helmet on, he's bowling F-ing quick!" and so the helmet got called for after three balls. He pitched a couple up and I thought, "This is alright," and then the next one went through throat-height and just missed my rather large hooter. That was an awakening, shall we say!'

As a player, Jim has a different take to the misty-eyed reminiscing of fans who hoovered up any and all cricket at Scarborough: 'I think the games that none of us particularly liked playing in was Yorkshire vs Old Yorkshiremen. We didn't really like those. Not that the opposition were bad, but we had everything to lose in that game.'

The Yorkshire vs The Yorkshiremen fixture first made its appearance in 1986 with Bill Athey, James Whitaker and Neil Mallender among those who came to North Yorkshire. The visitors comprised of county cricketers who had either played for Yorkshire or been born within its boundaries.

It was to reappear across 1989, 1990 and 1991, punctuated with the Yorkshire Exiles in 1988, which was the same concept in all but name. These novelties were won by Yorkshire, but not usually by very much; the odd few runs or wickets here or there.

* * *

The decline of the Festival is an unavoidable theme as it's much shorter and no longer hosts the touring international teams as it once did. I met up with David Warner, a respected journalist and friend who has been Editor of the Yorkshire County Cricket Club Yearbook for many years, to hear his Festival perspective and at what point this famous date in the summer calendar so dramatically shrunk.

He has recollections of the Fenner Trophy Final of 1972, three years before he started covering cricket professionally, that pitted Yorkshire against Lancashire. The home side triumphed by 60 runs in the 50-over contest, but a moment stood out.

'Lancashire batsman Jack Bond came out for his last innings in the Broad Acres and got a standing ovation right from coming out of the pavilion until he took his guard. There might have been 10,000 in the ground and they all stood as one. He was quite moved by it. Bond wasn't a great player, but he'd made himself into a gritty batsman and that's what they appreciated. That was a Lancashire captain, but it just showed the respect for him and what cricket means to the Yorkshire public.'

David sees the Festival as a meeting point for fans spread far and wide across Yorkshire. 'One of the things about watching cricket at Scarborough is that it brings together followers from all around the county, which you don't even get at Championship matches to such a degree. It's a slightly more relaxed mood, but yet they want to see the cricket played seriously.'

In the Fifties, it was still very competitive even in the T.N. Pearce's XI matches, because players like Fred Trueman and Bob Appleyard would require the occasional wicket or two to reach certain personal milestones that mattered a great deal.

For Warner, when he began his cricket journalism career in 1975, there were nine days of cricket in the Festival and it was launched with the Fenner Trophy one-day competition with Yorkshire beating Kent then losing to Hampshire several days later.

The programme of Festival cricket that year also included D.H. Robins' XI vs T.N. Pearce's XI and a Yorkshire side facing an International XI that Yorkshire won by seven wickets over three days. The county still had a trip to Middlesbrough to face Essex in the County Championship soon after, but there were the usual suspects at Scarborough of Boycott, Carrick, Hampshire, Bairstow and Old.

David's abiding memory of his debut season in the Scarborough press box was of a masterful spell of swing bowling by Tony Nicholson whose 5-45 included Brian

Close for a duck: 'He swung the ball more than I think I've seen anybody swing it. He didn't take a long run, but was very accurate. People will tell you who played with him, like Geoff Cope, that he was a master of swing.'

It was at this time when Championship cricket was invading into the space of the Festival, with Scarborough no longer guaranteed to be the icing on the cake at the end of a county season – and therefore Yorkshire not necessarily able to play a full part.

By 1995, it was still a relatively long Festival with ten days of cricket beginning with the touring West Indians and concluding with a County Championship match with Sussex; Scarborough had already hosted Worcestershire in early August for the Britannic Assurance County Championship.

But change was in the air and David observes how the Festival is now clutching onto some aspects of past traditions, with the band still present at games, but no longer playing such a central part where once the national anthem was belted out after each day's play in the 1950s.

In a similar vein, there's still a Festival dinner, but no longer the strictly black-tie affair at the Spa, so less chance of seeing a phalanx of penguins in town.

Ancillary events have also gone by the wayside as Scarborough Council used to welcome the team with an event in the Town Hall or Royal Hotel with the Mayor talking to the players. The schedule now, with counties zig-zagging across the country, doesn't allow for such social niceties; understandable, but a shame as the Festival no longer feels as immersive.

It's not just that there is less first-class cricket than there used to be, which obviously impacts who gets what. Yorkshire have seven home games and with York being awarded a Championship fixture in 2019 alongside Scarborough's allocation, there are only four at Headingley in Leeds. It's a delicate balancing act both for the fanbase in West Yorkshire and to please sponsors who've invested in a presence at the stadium.

It's where those cricket games fall that's the crux, with very little County Championship cricket in the middle section of the season, so any desire to mould two matches back-to-back at North Marine Road feels fanciful at best.

It's telling that from 1995 to 2005, the number of days of county cricket had been slashed in half. David and I are sat at a table in his home, surrounded by Yorkshire County Cricket Club Yearbooks and Wisden Almanacks. He checks before confirming the volume of county cricket in the Festival fell to just the Sussex four-dayer followed by a totesport League encounter with Derbyshire the next day by 2005.

If you're reading this wondering what all the fuss is about, it speaks to the worries about the future of the Festival and County Championship cricket more broadly. As we've seen, the trend for less four-day cricket is only going one way. It's a strange but awkward fact that four-day cricket commands an enormous popularity and audience online, allied with those who tune into live radio and TV broadcasts, yet that doesn't convert to bums on seats.

If the amount of Championship cricket at Scarborough can be halved in only a decade, it jangles alarm bells as to what the scene might be in 30 years from now. One way of ascertaining the health of the Festival is through crowd attendances and if it's warm and dry for a few days on the bounce then North Marine Road can be counted on to be packed out and as popular as any county ground in the country.

In 2015, the 129th Scarborough Cricket Festival spectators revelled in blue skies and the mercury dialled up as over 19,000 people came through the turnstiles over the four days. In the last ten years, Scarborough has frequently broken attendance records and punched well above its weight given its location and population of the region.

There is understandable pride in this and yet it's nothing compared to what crowds once were. The highest recorded attendance is believed to be 22,946 over only three days when Yorkshire played Derbyshire in 1947. Let that sink in for a moment. The official capacity of the same ground today is 11,500 and I've absolutely no idea how you would fit that many people inside. If you get 5,000 at North Marine Road, it looks like the place is fit to bursting.

Evidently, folk back then were much slimmer or comfortable standing nose to armpit with a near neighbour for eight hours. Photos of the 1950s show spectators in rows sat on the playing area in front of the Popular Bank so the boundary rope is even nearer to reach. Every square inch of space is filled.

What I can predict, with a fair degree of certainty, is that Scarborough Cricket Club would bite your hand off for an attendance like that in the future. However, that ship and that era have sailed.

The only way is Essex

When casting an eye back over the Scarborough Cricket Festival, more recent performances are inevitably fresher and ripe for excavation. There have been a couple of mammoth defeats for Yorkshire County Cricket Club over the last decade and the visit of Essex in 2017 was right up there. Of course, as Yorkshire fans will tell you with a nod and a wink, it was engineered by a couple of Yorkies.

Ex-Yorkshire & England all-rounder Anthony McGrath (known to many as 'Mags') was one of them and is well placed to reflect on the charms of Scarborough, having had a successful 17-year career for the county of his birth, before turning to coaching. Between 1995 and 2012, McGrath's 14,698 first-class runs at 36.83 and handy swing bowling (134 first-class wickets at 35.66) made him a regular for the White Rose.

When we caught up by phone, those softly spoken Bradfordian tones didn't take long to wax lyrical: 'Scarborough's one of my favourite grounds in England, second only to Lord's. I've always loved going, I watched as a youngster and then I got to play there.'

McGrath's debut representing his county at North Marine Road was against the West Indians on September

3, 1995, where he opened with Simon Kellett and hit his first List A century (106).

He recalls the first time he walked out for Yorkshire at Scarborough. 'Coming out to bat, it really struck me how close the crowd were to the pitch. Having been in the ground and watched it, to being out in the middle to look around, it was just incredible. We batted second and the Popular Bank had had plenty to drink; the noise was really loud. I just remember them getting behind me as a young player and getting a few runs was a memorable day.'

He returned to the Yorkshire coast against Somerset in their Britannic Assurance County Championship match of July 1996. It did not go well. A whirlwind innings of 134 off 109 balls from Australian Shane Lee set Yorkshire a target of 413 in 127 overs to win. McGrath notched up his first 'king pair' in first-class cricket by top-edging a pull and was caught by third slip for his second innings of the match without troubling the scorers.

However, the 1996 Scarborough Cricket Festival and specifically the McCain Challenge, where Yorkshire took on a Tesco International XI, was to prove more profitable. McGrath top-scored with 106 in a three-wicket win. It was to be a productive few days as he hit a breezy 54 off 34 balls the next day in the 50-over Northern Electric Trophy where Yorkshire beat Durham by 45 runs.

The cricket came thick and fast back then. A day later, the visiting Netherlands uncharitably won their McCain Challenge match by three wickets before Yorkshire thrashed Durham by 123 runs in the semi-final of the Tetley

Bitter Festival. The Final saw McGrath get a bowl at last, albeit three expensive overs as Yorkshire tried eight bowlers, but it was a David Byas hundred that saw them home.

As we hone in on what Scarborough Cricket Club means to him, thoughts turned to how North Marine Road had reinvented itself after a string of draws on lifeless, batsman-friendly surfaces.

'It used to be a pretty batsman-friendly wicket, but since they re-laid it, it's a really, really good cricket wicket. It normally carries through, a lot of pace and if you do go through the four days, it normally turns. I remember Adil Rashid making his debut and the third and fourth days, it really turned sharply. If you speak to the players nowadays who play there, they put it down as one of the best wickets around.'

McGrath was to return to Scarborough in 2017 as Assistant Coach of Essex County Cricket Club (since promoted to Head Coach after Chris Silverwood left the county to become England bowling coach).

What followed was a helter-skelter two days that culminated in one of Yorkshire's most harrowing County Championship defeats. The first day saw 18 wickets fall with Mohammad Amir (5-18) at the fore and Essex led by 75 runs with two first-innings wickets remaining. I still remember it with a shudder, but watching from the pavilion, what had McGrath made of it?

The word he chooses to use is 'surreal' which is as good as any. It was something of a homecoming as his family and friends were there and obviously familiar faces in the Yorkshire set-up. I wondered what it was like as a Yorkshireman, returning to his county where McGrath had been a mainstay, now plotting its downfall?

Players and coaches do what it takes to get the job done, but there's something more personal in sport and this wasn't any old victory but a proper hammering. I suspect there isn't time to dwell on margins of victory in any format as long as the points are in the bag. Compartmentalisation can help lend perspective too:

'It was the first time I'd been back to the club, so great to see familiar faces, but once we got underway, professionalism really takes over. I was just focussed on getting a win for Essex.

'We'd done prep on the Yorkshire players, but with myself and Chris (Silverwood) having played at Scarborough many times, we had that insight of how the wicket was going to play. We know at Scarborough you have to bowl that little bit fuller than most places with the new ball and that's what we did. I think Jamie Porter and Mohammad Amir were absolutely superb that game. We were right on top from the first few overs. That game gave us the belief we could go on and win the Championship.'

He didn't attribute anything remotely untoward with the pitch over that helter-skelter, 48-hour period, crediting the quality of the bowling instead, but coastal conditions can play their part. As you'll hear more than once, the conditions at Scarborough can be a law unto themselves, oscillating between a baked deck for batsmen to gorge themselves and a seaming serpent when the sea fret drifts inland.

'It just depended on what kind of day it was and the weather forecast. I remember being (Yorkshire) captain there a few times when the old fret was in, in the morning, and when you bowled, it really swung around all over the place. As soon as the sun came through, it flattened out. Similarly, towards the end of a day, it (the fret) could come in for the last hour and make it difficult to bat. I've played in games where if the sun's out all day, the second and third day is absolute paradise to bat because it's small boundaries and once it beats in the infield, it's four runs.'

Forgive me, Yorkshire fans, for dwelling on a painful recent defeat at Scarborough. But, it interested me what that particular game was like for those directly involved, not least a Yorkshireman the North Marine Road crowd would know well. It was also a litmus test of the strength of feeling for the Festival. Can performance on the field ruin the seaside reverie off it?

To some extent, the crowds at Scarborough haven't changed over all this time. There was always a desire to see a Yorkshire win, but as long as entertainment was there, it couldn't dampen the holiday mood. Sure, those I spoke to after the Essex game were horrified at the speed of Yorkshire's batting collapses, but most went away aware that they had witnessed something special in Mohammad Amir.

* * *

Of course, Mohammad Amir's story is one of a promising international career, subsequent bad decisions and possible redemption, following his five-year ban by the International Cricket Council (ICC) for involvement in a spot-fixing betting scandal.

By bowling two deliberate no-balls in the 2010 Lord's Test against England, he set off a chain of events that snipped five years from his career and ruined his reputation. Amir was subsequently restored to Pakistan's national side and has since proved capable of moments of match-altering sorcery with hostile pace and malevolent swing.

Amir's recruitment by Essex was a brief headline, but it paid off; though the grunt work and reward were shared by Jamie Porter's seamers and Simon Harmer's off-spin, whose 147 wickets between them propelled Essex to their first County Championship in a quarter of a century.

Notably, there were no catcalls hurled in Amir's direction during that Scarborough match. I vaguely recall some joker shouting out 'No ball!' from the crowd, but that was hardly original. Whether he should have been banned for life or not, in a very uncomplicated Yorkshire way, Amir had served his time. 'Fair play to that Amir,' or, 'That lad Amir's not bad, is he?' were both overheard at North Marine Road and as fulsome praise as you could wish for.

As for Essex, they had been Yorkshire's bogey team in 2017, handing out punishments home and away. After Amir's ten-wicket showstopper at Scarborough, Essex won the return leg by 376 runs at Chelmsford, but 2018 turned out to include a dramatic reverse in fortunes.

Despite containing three of the top-ten ranked batsmen in Root, Bairstow and Pujara, Yorkshire were rolled over for 50 down at Essex in May. Harry Brook's first County Championship hundred in the second innings was followed by Steve Patterson's six wickets to engineer an extraordinary 91-run victory.

It was a match that Yorkshire had no right to win and at first glance, were being frogmarched to defeat after an extraordinary 20 wickets fell before tea on the first day. Essex led by 92 runs on first innings and were eventually set 238 to win, but it proved too much. Those are the kind of matches that lurch this way and that, defying predictions and making fools of pundits.

Anthony McGrath, who has just about seen it all in his brief coaching spell, called it a 'crazy game' in echoes of that scintillating Scarborough Cricket Festival match of 2017. When it comes to the two counties, it's usually best to buckle up for a ride.

Storm clouds and sea frets in June

The news in May 2018 that India's captain Virat Kohli was heading to Surrey for the month of June was met with almost as much excitement in Wakefield as in Woking. For Yorkshire fans, it meant that one of the sport's truly global superstars would be ending his stint in county cricket a stone's throw from Peasholm Park.

Note the use of past tense, but we'll come to that in a second. County Championship cricket fans often have a love-hate relationship with the Indian Premier League (IPL); you need look no further than the reaction to the way that David Willey and Liam Plunkett left Yorkshire County Cricket Club's pre-season plans in some disarray when they joined IPL franchises at late notice.

It's not a stretch to see why four-day cricket in England comes a distant second for players, after the glamour and wages of the IPL – and the curse of T20 struck again. No sooner were the marketing teams at county clubs salivating, than the news filtered through that Virat would no longer be wearing the whites of Surrey after all.

A neck injury while fielding at the M. Chinnaswamy

Stadium in Bengaluru during a VIVO IPL match between Royal Challengers Bangalore and Sunrisers Hyderabad had put paid to his maiden appearance in county cricket.

While a little of the stardust had been sprinkled and then hastily put away again, Surrey's Specsavers County Championship fixture at Scarborough in the last week of June 2018 retained its blockbuster status.

Surrey were purring along in four-day cricket and already had the tag of favourites for the title. Though not the Scarborough Cricket Festival fixture itself, the visit of Surrey was either an appetiser or the untimely main course. Would it enhance the chatter about Scarbados or absorb some of its radiance?

Surrey arrived as Championship leaders and the team to unseat, with South African giant Morne Morkel in their ranks; primed to exploit the steep bounce that once made Jason Gillespie liken Scarborough to the Waroona clay pitches of the WACA in Perth.

As much as the afternoon sea breeze (nicknamed the 'Fremantle Doctor') sweeps in across the shoreline of Western Australia, we were to be reminded of the coastal quirks of North Marine Road on day two against Surrey. First, Yorkshire recovered from 166-6 to be dismissed for 337 as Jonathan Tattersall (70) and Tim Bresnan (48) took their time to blunt everything Surrey threw at them.

The second day saw Surrey end proceedings peering into a Stygian gloom. Play concluded early as the sea fret that had ghosted in transformed the cricket ground to a murky scene from Victorian London. There was even time for a welcome Yorkshire bonus as Mark Stoneman's frustrated reaction to being caught behind, allied with another incident by a Surrey player, led to the rarity of a five-run penalty, with Yorkshire's total topped up to 342.

I was following the game back home in West Yorkshire to catch a few overs from the Yorkshire coast. This was a unique partnership between the counties with the live stream given the green light by Sky Sports, who own the TV broadcast rights to all international and county matches in England.

Live streaming (real-time broadcasting over the internet) is not new in cricket but typically, it's from a single fixed camera, or two if you're lucky. Viewers don't get the panoramic, 360-degree experience we all take for granted with professional broadcasters. Of course, they don't have to pay a hefty subscription fee either.

Having no sound, or a radio commentary that doesn't marry with the pictures, is not something to get wildly excited about so this was a marked improvement. It featured four cameras and a BBC radio feed synced with the pictures. Having interviewed the analysts at Yorkshire County Cricket Club years back, I knew that all the counties had cameras fitted at each end to record matches, so that players could watch back and the data be crunched for insight.

It struck me back then, and we're talking about a decade ago, that this was a missed opportunity, if the footage was already being captured. Perhaps the quality of streaming wasn't what it is now or Sky Sports were more truculent in hoarding their sports rights.

No matter – if you couldn't be there at Scarborough, in the middle of a searing heatwave that had settled over the country and refused to budge, the free live feed on the Yorkshire and Surrey county websites was a welcome companion.

If hope sprang eternal as Yorkshire gained a first innings lead, it was extinguished after they were hurried out the second time around for 152. While my focus is typically on writing about clubs and league cricket, I'd seen enough of Yorkshire to know that a brittle top order continue to be bailed out by their potent bowling attack.

Surrey advanced to 89-0 in their pursuit of 228 and appeared to be cruising towards the fifth win of their Division One campaign, but you just never know. Yorkshire required early and regular wickets on the final day and perhaps another sea fret to spice up the wicket. As it turned out, they got neither.

What interested me, given how Scarborough is heralded and cherished, was the reaction to the prices for day four. Unless Surrey folded like a deckchair then there would be a session or half a day's play at most – but pricing was kept at £16 for an adult and £5 for a junior.

Cue outrage on Twitter, admittedly not the most level-headed of discussion forums. I felt compelled to defend the county club as the costs to Scarborough Cricket Club don't diminish notably if play finishes early. I remember a cafe in Liverpool, now no more tellingly, that charged its customers based on the time spent. They could partake in as much tea, coffee and Wi-Fi as they liked.

Wouldn't it be interesting to run an experiment where spectators at a county game could pay on the gate whatever they felt was appropriate? Or, what they felt reflected the quality of cricket? It's not a business model I'd advocate, but as a bit of social engineering, what might be the results?

Would we all overpay if Yorkshire were delivering high-octane feats of utter brilliance? Would we underpay when there is a fervent cry to defend the County Championship and all the cost that involves? I don't have any of the answers, I'm just stoking the fire.

What we're prepared to pay for and where we expect a discount is a subject that interests me both as a journalist creating content and the business owner of a website that distributes it for free. We are so awash with freebies and discounts that paying full price – albeit for a truncated day – can be an anathema. How much does it cost to go to the cinema or theatre for 90 minutes of entertainment?

That reaction about the last day at Scarborough, where an unpalatable result appeared to be already etched in stone, tapped into the strategy of Test matches lowering prices on the final day. I suspect the dying embers of the Surrey game wasn't watched from the stands by all that many, but the question of whether to lower prices on final days must vex those at county clubs.

Surrey serenely cruised to a seven-wicket win with Rory Burns contributing 97 and Scott Borthwick quashing any hopes for a Yorkshire fightback with 62. It cemented Surrey's lead at the top and though Yorkshire had led the match by 75 runs, the spectre of the third innings, where they were 42-4 before lunch on day three, would torment for a while.

Though the fulsome media attention on county cricket at Scarborough in the national press was lavish, there was a rare moment to bring us all crashing down. Surrey complained to the England & Wales Cricket Board (ECB) after one of their players (tentatively named in the press as all-rounder Ryan Patel) was alleged to have been racially abused by a member of the crowd.

To say 'alleged' is to wait until the investigations have been concluded, still awaited as this book goes to print almost one year down the line. With no-one individually accused and few witnesses, a satisfying conclusion always felt unlikely, but something clearly happened.

As far as I understand it, nothing was seen by other spectators and no-one was apprehended, though the club did have plain-clothes spotters in place soon after to try to identify the culprit – without luck.

It's very difficult to pick out someone in the crowd in the heat of the moment unless they're seen at that time and it's up to those around to get involved. Cricket matches don't have the same police presence as football after all.

If I was to level any criticism, it would be that this has taken far too long. There will be a process and due diligence in something as serious as this. You can't rush the pursuit of the facts – and yet, we had still heard nothing a year later. To my mind, it sent out entirely the wrong message of a lack of priority – though no blame lies with either county club or the venue given it was out of their hands.

The knowledge and passion of the crowds at Scarborough has made it such a favourite for cricketers down the years; the intimacy of the amphitheatre by the sea and the passion of the Yorkshire faithful sends a spark down the back of the neck. We'd hope this was an isolated, if depressing, occasion, but there can only be one response – to call out and punish racism in all forms.

It has happened before at Scarborough. Back in the Eighties, the Gloucestershire fast bowler David 'Syd' Lawrence had bananas thrown at him as he was fielding. These events are rare – but not unheard of – and it's how the game responds that acutely matters.

There is no place for it and it really saddened me that, of all the cricket grounds where I might have imagined such a thing would happen, Scarborough never came to mind – but it only takes one idiot.

Arriving in Scarborough: Paradise and mushy peas

After months of seeing the 132nd Scarborough Cricket Festival as a mirage shimmering on the horizon, it arrives out of nowhere. It is Saturday morning at Leeds train station and the 10.21 to Scarborough on platform 15b is nowhere near as packed as it will be on the day of the game itself.

The journey towards York is quiet and uneventful with the occasional high-pitched yelp from any number of small dogs who are in the carriage. A woman with hair the colour of purple pansies cools herself with an oriental paper fan.

I allow my mind to wander, watching a silent movie of the landscape around Church Fenton rush by outside. It has been a breathless few weeks for The Yorkshire County Cricket Club.

It has always struck me as somewhat ironic that 'The' is an integral part of the club's identity when the region has never much bothered with this popular, inter-connecting word. Hearing 'wife is on bus' is one of life's joys for a surrogate Yorkie.

I am fortunate to know a number of people who can fill

in historical context and so it was that author Mick Pope emailed to clarify that the minutes of the Yorkshire CCC constitution from January 8, 1863, at the Adelphi Hotel, Sheffield read: 'That a County Club be formed, the Annual Subscription to be not less than 10/6 per member.'

I had always assumed that it was there in black and white, contractually speaking, but it must have evolved in part because there was inter-city jostling between factions at the time of the formation of the county club.

In language, 'the' is a definite article; a moment of emphasis, and yet, on the other hand, it's one of the most common words in English. It's always felt a little pompous to refer to the cricket club as the best and yet only version of itself.

No matter, Yorkshire had a flurry of squad-related news with opening batsman Alex Lees departing immediately to Durham, all-rounder Tim Bresnan signing a new two-year contract to the end of 2020, pace bowler Jack Brooks in talks with Somerset over a possible move, England's Liam Plunkett off to Surrey and Warwickshire leg-spinner Josh Poysden moving to the White Rose county.

You'd think that was enough, but club captain Steve Patterson had broken the forefinger in his left hand, ruling him out for weeks, and New Zealand international batsman Jeet Raval had signed for Yorkshire for the remainder of the 2018 season, initially as injury cover for Kane Williamson.

Of course, such machinations will be old news long before you read this, and yet, the helter-skelter hinted of trouble at mill and spoke of a county cutting its cloth accordingly after housing numerous England internationals whose availability was ever-more infrequent.

Signings at Yorkshire always polarise opinion, but it would not be unkind to suggest that only county fans with an ardent grasp of international cricket would know much about Jeet Raval. A cursory Google would reveal the video clip of Raval striking a maximum for Auckland where the ball hit bowler Andrew Ellis but flew for six.

Still, as we clattered our way ever closer to Scarborough, headlines mischievously popped into my head. It was surely a matter of time before 'Jeet reet sweet treat.'

An overseas signing for the last weeks of the County Championship suggested a worry that Yorkshire might be pulled into a relegation scrap during September. Similarly, in 2017, the county had secured West Indies Test batsman Kraigg Brathwaite for the final two games of the County Championship season after hitting 134 and 95 in the Test at Headingley.

There will always be those that prefer a home-grown player being given time to prove himself over a signing from another county or country, and yet, when push comes to shove, the county remaining in Division One is sacrosanct.

In retrospect, Raval's stint was not to include headline-hoovering scores, but a recommendation from Kane Williamson, one of the best Test batsmen of his generation, had clearly carried weight.

We haven't even got to the controversy over Adil Rashid renouncing his desire to play red-ball, four-day cricket for Yorkshire, only to be picked by England's Test team and therefore miss the culmination of Yorkshire's T20 Vitality Blast qualification bid – the only form of cricket his county had been able to sign him for.

An unedifying soap opera that Yorkshire might have nipped in the bud by refusing Rashid a white-ball contract (but world-class leggies don't grow on trees) or if England had forced him to play for Yorkshire in the conveniently scheduled four-day derby at Old Trafford, just before the first Test between England and India at Edgbaston.

This and plenty more besides came to mind as the landscape scrolled speedily by. I pondered how many captains Yorkshire had managed to get through in the season with Gary Ballance relinquishing the reins to Steve Patterson, whose injury now meant David Willey was likely to be the third captain in the County Championship in five months.

Joe Root had actually taken charge for the innings defeat at Surrey back in May and Adam Lyth would lead for the trip to Trent Bridge in September, making it up to five in only 13 games. If you're curious, the record, brought to you by the unerring research of Yorkshire author Paul Dyson, was six captains. Though that was back in 1923 and there had been 23 matches that year.

Meanwhile, to lend a little context leading into the Scarborough Cricket Festival, Yorkshire had just crashed out of the T20 competition the night before. Alex Hales belted 71 as the defending champions, Nottingham Outlaws, won by eight wickets and Yorkshire Vikings finished fifth in the North group.

It meant that their last chance of silverware had been snuffed out before the knockout stages. Still, Yorkshire were targeting a top-three finish in first-class cricket, whereas Worcestershire were bottom and desperately needing a win at North Marine Road.

The T20 defeat by Nottinghamshire Outlaws at Headingley had precipitated a predictable torrent of abuse aimed at the players as well as coach Andrew Gale and Director of Cricket Martyn Moxon. A hashtag on Twitter of #GaleOut was gaining some traction and I caught a few glances in my direction on the train as I had an inner dialogue, shook my head and sighed deeply to myself.

I am of the view, old-fashioned it might be, that we are all responsible for our opinions. Yet, the age of social media has given an outlet for snap verdicts, divorced from any considered thought or fact. To pluck an example, a bloke who's had a terrible day at work can sit in his pants with a laptop on his knee and rattle off 280 characters of unrestrained bile, bluntly directed at another human being.

The more chilling variant is that he has had a stellar day, but believes that his favourite cricket team is being managed by the devil incarnate. In fact, with the likes of Facebook and Twitter only requiring an age limit of over 13, it could just as easily be a teenage girl. Or an angry granny.

The point is not that anyone is wrong to voice their view,

as cricket followers have as much right as any to hold their team to account. It's just a frustration that so often everything is sunshine and smiles and, in the next instant, the world is caving in and everyone should be sacked.

Fortunes in cricket can oscillate quickly, but it never ceases to astonish me what is written and put out into the world, publicly searchable in Google, fully attributable to a person who has kindly supplied a profile picture and given their real name for good measure.

As I work myself up, our train has come to a halt outside Malton with the engine running and vibrations making my teeth chatter.

Moira has joined me for this week and we're on a TransPennine Express train; a look around its faux wood fold-down tables and blue patchwork upholstery is to observe that it has been refurbished. In all of my extensive travel around Yorkshire and the Humber, it is the only company that has yet upgraded its trains.

Counting against that praise, we are on a route spanning Liverpool and Hull and up to North Yorkshire that is woefully inadequate for the demand placed upon it on a daily basis. That rail rant is for another time, and perhaps another book, but suffice to say that a commute between Leeds and Manchester or cross-country to Hull is not for the claustrophobic during peak time.

We get moving again and a daydream or two later, we are almost at Seamer. The inspector takes my Two Together tickets and then hands them back with a reverential, 'Your tickets, Mr Fuller.' He has clocked the name on the railcard, but even so, it's a first and the lingering sense of importance, however brief, is appreciated.

* * *

Scarborough railway station is jammed. As our train gives a final respiratory judder and comes to rest, a wall of travellers keen to get a seat on the journey back to Liverpool Lime Street peer in, as if an army of the undead in a zombie movie.

A plucky employee from the train company demands everyone on the platform takes a step back so we can all leave in something approaching an orderly fashion. As a column snakes its way outside, the first insistent decibels of seagulls greet us. I cannot fully savour the moment as I usually do. I have one eye protectively on the blind man in front of us; tapping the floor with his white cane and rollerball tip, as those behind me peer around my shoulder to see what the hold up is.

We opt for lunch and duck into a botanical-themed eatery called The Garden Shed near the station, tempted in by its realistic flowers hanging en masse from the ceiling – and where else can you eat in Scarborough with a selection of gardening tools on the walls as trophies?

After a decadent break, a group of bikers who congregated outside on Victoria Road with their engines running, spewing petrol fumes into the cafe, persuaded us that it was time to move on and find our temporary home by the sea.

North Bay Guest House is one of many bed and breakfasts on Columbus Ravine; a short section of the A165 that sweeps down to the edge of Peasholm Park and then continues on its way to the village of Burniston, North of the town.

Greeted by owner John, our room was ready at the top of the property and we had everything we needed. Online reviews had come up trumps; it's little wonder North Bay is so well thought of and even has a wall of thank you cards from guests pinned up downstairs.

We got the latest gossip about Britney Spears' performance at Scarborough Open Air Theatre. For the first but not the last time during the trip, the feedback was damning. With tickets costing at least £125 each, the observation that she appeared to mime rather than sing did not go down well in Yorkshire.

We ambled along to Scarborough Cricket Club to put up posters promoting this very book and asking for fans to come forward with their own Festival narratives. There had been a fevered discussion in the Fuller household as to the design of said posters.

Ultimately, my one-woman PR department had won out and a sizeable photo of the author was included. I thought I might be mistaken as an advert for a Where's Wally? competition but they actually proved to be very effective; not least because Mrs Fuller planned to cover every inch of North Marine Road.

* * *

To walk through the gates at Scarborough Cricket Club is to feel the worries of the world slip from your shoulders. This particular Saturday saw the ground lit beautifully with the glow of afternoon sunshine. Even without any cricket, it's a marvel and we stood for a moment; each lost in our own thoughts. Moira had never seen the ground before and was the first to break the silence:

'Isn't this amazing? It's incredible that they let anyone just wander in.'

We weren't the only ones there. A number of cricket fans or curious tourists stood in small groups absorbing the aura of this little amphitheatre, hidden from view by terraced housing. Scarborough Seconds were due to be at home to Woodhouse Grange in the York & District Senior Cricket League, but the fixture had been moved to Scarborough College to allow for Festival preparations.

Indulge me, as I take you on a tour of the ground. I'd suggest you close your eyes to encourage the map in your mind's eye, but that might make reading this part of the chapter a little onerous unless someone reads it to you.

Looking left from the entrance, your eye follows the curve of the wooden benches that make up the Popular Bank running down to pitchside without any barrier whatsoever. The end of this portion of the ground is punctuated by the Tea Room; one of the landmarks of North Marine Road.

I've only ever seen its distinctive bold lettering across the roof, that loudly expresses tea and cake, at Delph and

Dobcross Cricket Club in the Huddersfield Cricket League – but it speaks to another age. Though Scarborough's tea room has been upgraded and modernised, I like that they've left this feature untouched and it remains a memorable reference point.

Behind, running right along that side of the ground, are the backs of the terraced houses on Trafalgar Square, painted shades of cream, brown and grey with a mishmash of windows at assorted levels. If those houses could talk, eh? They've been bombarded with sixes for more than a century. There are so many stories of how the ball has shattered windows or even gone through an opening into one of the boarding houses. It is quite a strike to belt it that far.

At the Trafalgar Square End of the cricket ground, there's a stretch of plastic seating, split by the sightscreen, with the Bill Foord Enclosure favoured by members furthest down. It's named after the fast-medium bowler whose 51 first-class matches for Yorkshire between 1947 and 1953 saw him take 126 wickets.

Bill's playing career at North Marine Road covered 30 years from 1941 to 1971 and his record of 1,071 wickets at an average of 15.07 marks him out as one of the club's finest bowlers. Latterly, he promoted the junior game by funding and coaching in a scholarship scheme to support young Scarborough cricketers.

The naming of parts of a cricket ground after its stalwarts is not something done lightly, but is a posthumous accolade that I find touching as the name lives on and is spoken over many years by future generations. I'd like to think there's a club ground somewhere in Yorkshire that one day has a bench with a little brass nod to the thousands of hours I've spent scoffing my face at tea.

Directly opposite is the West Stand; a no-frills block of uncovered seating with a side-on view of the cricket. A marquee is to the left of the block, where invited guests sit down to lunch, or wander outside and plonk themselves in a striped deckchair to catch a few overs.

Gazebos were being erected as I continued my visual sweep, with the North Stand on our right at the Peasholm Park end of the ground. Here, you can sample a day of Championship cricket from behind the bowler's arm, with the banked seating stretching much higher than the sightscreen.

The Press Box is part of the North Stand, where journalists and scorers share a single, glass-fronted headquarters; two smaller homes for broadcasting sit adjacent but separate next door, resembling garden sheds.

At the side of the North Stand closest to us, the pavilion at Scarborough is the defining feature and draws the eye; the red brick edifice with a balcony that stretches the full length of the upper floor was built in 1896 for the princely sum of £2,150. To look at a photograph from the 1924 Festival with the MCC squad half posing, half scowling outside is to realise that little has changed in its appearance from the outside.

In an era of modern stadiums, the ground stands out as being of a time long gone but fondly remembered. The aesthetic matches the rest of the relaxed approach to cricket at Scarborough.

Players taking the field from the pavilion have to walk through a central aisle between the county members' seats, with a white staircase behind that connects to a lounge indoors.

In J.M. Kilburn's seminal 1948 book on the Scarborough Cricket Festival, there's a black and white photo of the old pavilion with the Scarborough XI of 1874. The one-level wooden structure cost £400, with the image conjuring up a wild west saloon but for a scorer pictured in a black hat and the scoreboard showing 120-10 off 21 overs.

Signage at Scarborough subtly plays its part in reminding everyone who visits that they are part of a Scarbadian time warp. It's a world away from Headingley or the Ageas Bowl. The 'Players Only' in black capital letters on a white sign decrees the sacred space of the Yorkshire changing room. Use of the right font and colour is an art the more you look around.

The final part of this 360-degree tour is to mention the cricket ground boundary wall along North Marine Road that runs back towards the main entrance gate. The Yorkshire Cricket Foundation charity usually have their mobile museum parked with exhibits to muse at. For the past couple of years, there has also been a pop-up pizza place, complete with oven fired up, that ensures the waft of stone baked temptation is never far from the nostrils.

Behind this hive of activity are three plaques that could

be easily missed but capture a snapshot of salient historical facts.

The round navy blue Scarborough Heritage Trail notes that Scarborough Cricket Club was founded in 1849 and on this site since 1863. Next is the stone plaque in the shape of a shield that was put up in 1878 to commemorate the purchase of this cricket ground in that year for the sum of £7,000.

The bottom half has long since weathered away, but it's possible to make out the trustees, starting with Right Honorable Lord Londesborough. A third, more recent white square plaque with gold trim next to it clarifies the dates and purchase sum.

Mrs Fuller and I stand next to the black signpost near the entrance gates, another landmark of sorts that identifies the ground to those who have an affinity with the place. With a nod to both practical and humour, the Pavilion Members bar points off one way, as does the destination of Durham's county ground of Riverside Chester-le-Street at 84.6 miles. Lord's and Headingley also feature among more localised destinations.

Groundsman John Dodds is out in the middle with his faded navy Scarborough Cricket Club polo shirt and tanned arms reflecting the unusual ferocity of this British summer heat. In a moment reflecting the times in which we live, he is filming a pitch report on his mobile phone to publish later on Twitter.

He hops onto a blue tractor to drag the green domed covers off the square and a high-pitched squeak comically follows him as the ground equipment snakes its way towards the West Stand.

We catch up out in the middle and John, who has been groundsman at North Marine Road since 2011, wears an enormous grin as he recalls his first visit here as a boy.

First ball of the morning, Fred Trueman was bowling at the Australian batsman Bobby Simpson who guided the ball down to the corner by the tea room for four. The next ball ended up there too, but Simpson was out as Trueman had sent his stump cartwheeling. Dodds remembers that it went spinning, groove over spike, most of the way to the boundary.

With the Yorkshire players beginning to arrive and a promise secured to talk to Dodds during the Festival, we decide to explore the rest of Scarborough on foot.

* * *

Back towards the town centre from the cricket ground is a roundabout and the fish and chips emporium of Rennards. It's a popular lunchtime destination for cricket fans who shirk the in-stadium catering in favour of battered haddock down the way.

It's quiet by 3pm and, to the bemusement of the rest of the staff, I lean against the counter and talk to the owner who gives an insight into how an early finish at the cricket affects trade. In 2017, when Yorkshire were tonked by Essex inside two days, Rennards had ordered their usual quota of fish to feed hundreds of fans over four days, but were left counting the cost to the tune of 20 stone of surplus.

A cheerier tale follows with a hazy memory of a one-dayer decades back, when a bumper crowd meant they ran out of fish and had to put in an emergency call to their supplier who initially raised their prices, but ended up giving it over for free.

Again, I hear that cricket at Scarborough is not like it used to be and is not really a festival anymore. Both are absolutely true and from the perspective of a fish and chip shop or a bed and breakfast owner, the reality that a two-week festival became a ten-day festival then gradually a four-day game is bound to have ramifications.

That being said, such is the demand here in peak season that the fluctuations of the ECB's scheduling doesn't really hurt the tourist trade's bottom line. Threading through the town, I opt to take Moira back to Greensmith & Thackwray on St Nicholas Street, the former outfitter turned cafe, for some cake and to watch the world go by.

As the coffee machine splutters into life, Aretha Franklin's soundtrack 'Respect' bounces off the walls; a tribute in the week that the American singer-songwriter died. A lad on crutches hobbles past on the other side of the street. Each crutch is festooned with mini Yorkshire paper flags, so he is shuffling and fluttering at the same time.

Cricket is rarely from my thoughts and it often finds me in the oddest of places. The toilet at Greensmith & Thackwray has a black and white photo of the cafe's front, back when it was a shop, with a sign for the 46th Scarborough Cricket Festival in the window.

We amble back outside and, further along the road, spot a cricket bat, priced £15, leaning in the corner of a closed shop called The Vintage Window. It is a 'Captain Special' and has been made in Pakistan. The surface of the bat is littered with pockmarks; crescent-shaped indentations that reflect a life well used.

It's a rare cricketing find among Star Wars toys (if only I'd kept hold of my Millennium Falcon spaceship) and older items from the past hundred years. I like the way the blue-painted window frames curve around as if each is its own cabinet of curiosities. Near the bat is what appears to be a sink plunger with a copper top, a black and white railway sign for Scarborough and a plastic foot.

We decide to dip into the Grand Hotel, once the tourism epicentre of the town and still an arresting sight perched on St Nicholas Cliff.

The Grand used to be the finest place in Scarborough to stay, dine and be seen. It had a Cricketers' Room with photos of amateur players adorning the walls where it would host the teams, but times have radically changed since it was sold to Butlins in 1978.

As we push through the doors of the hotel, we are greeted by utter bedlam. There's a horseshoe-shaped queue stretching right around the foyer to one desk where two flustered employees are doing their best to serve what must be a line of a hundred unimpressed guests as quickly as possible. The twinkle of lights and attention-seeking tunes from the array of arcade machines in the foyer give uncomfortable background music to those waiting.

We head past the bar, and another whopper of a queue, to go out onto the verandah where huge seagulls land on tables and waddle towards us menacingly. The views are a treat with the full stretch of South Bay beach before us and the crashing waves from the North Sea rushing in and retreating.

Back outside the hotel, the winding decline through St Nicholas Gardens with its palm leaves and bursts of floral colour takes us down to the South Bay promenade for a walk about the harbour. We then stretch our hamstrings on the climb up to St Mary's Church where the novelist and poet Anne Brontë is buried.

It's peaceful up here, just below Scarborough Castle, and a world removed from the flashing lights and typical seaside attractions that have brought the crowds out below. After the hill, we pause to catch our breath and realise that we've stumbled upon 'Paradise.'

It's the name of a street in Scarborough's Old Town that includes an enclosed ornamental garden and a gap in the red brick wall that affords a lingering look out to sea. We find our way back to North Marine Road and on a whim, opt for the home comforts of North Bay Cafe on the corner. Without realising it at the time, this will become a popular haunt in the coming days.

It would not be a disservice to the clientele to note that, by and large, we are the youngest diners by a good few decades. Everything about it feels dated, but that is fully intended as a compliment. Twenty-first century cafe chains are transient, impersonal places where choice comes with a hefty price and eating and drinking feels functional at best.

For convenience's sake, there is such a place that I sometimes frequent in Leeds railway station. You only get a plastic cup. There is nowhere to deposit your tea bag, so I end up tutting loudly and dumping it in a napkin. It leaches into the soft tissue as if a sepia print developing in a darkroom. You can choose 43 varieties of coffee, but Earl Grey is the only other option of tea and that is seen as exotic. For a nation of tea drinkers, I can't help but feel that's the wrong way round.

Here in Scarborough, North Bay Cafe is busy with those having supper and we slide into a booth by the door and inspect the menu. They know their audience here, with an entire section devoted to large Yorkshire pudding (note the emphasis on size) filled with beef gravy, mash, chicken curry or anything you can possibly think of.

The baby blue painted walls and pink and purple chequered tablecloths lift the decor, though the counter where customers go to order has a white 'Counter Service' sign in red lettering that parks North Bay Cafe in the Eighties or even earlier. As if to emphasise the point, 'Summer Holiday' by Cliff Richard and The Shadows floats over the radio.

There's another notable observation. It runs the risk of appearing as if I plan to frequently describe aspects of toilets around Scarborough, but I will press on. There's a hand dryer downstairs in the loos optimistically called 'The Magnum.' It was probably installed at the time of the first Scarborough Cricket Festival.

Perfectly encapsulating the whole Scarborough ethos that sometimes change isn't necessary, it belts out hot air with the enthusiasm of a flame-thrower suffering from a persistent dry cough. It has a comically large red button that summons up images of heads of government sweating in their office clutching nuclear codes.

My battered haddock and chips comes with mushy peas that are radioactive green and very tasty. Everything is served quickly with a smile and is ideal comfort food. Besides, any meal deal that includes bread and butter and a mug of tea has my name on it and the reasonable prices speak to my inner Yorkshireman.

* * *

Later that evening, we decide to explore the Hollywood Plaza cinema across the road from the North Bay Cafe. It has seen better days and would benefit from a lick of paint. Nonetheless, as an independent, its charm lies in being an alternative experience to a typical multiplex, beginning with the old-fashioned, individually placed red letters above the entrance door that announce which films are showing.

In the spirit of adventure, we pick a movie, find seats near the front and wait for the film to start. The Hollywood Plaza is celebrating its 100-year anniversary and the seats could well be the originals, judging by the way I'm hunched forward like a curious praying mantis. It must be my height or weight distribution, but I struggled to keep the seat flat. It kept wanting to eat me.

As I sighed, swapped seats and swapped back again, a lad stood stock-still at the front with confectionery in a 1950s-style tray. No-one stepped forward to buy and in the half-gloom, it was as if he was the last pick on a sports team. I felt like I should leap forward and buy a bag of popcorn. If only. I was still in the clutches of a half-closed clam masquerading as a cinema seat.

A rolled-up jumper at my back seemed to address my equilibrium problems and we sat through a film about an ant-man and a wasp. It was standard Hollywood fare, but the visit had been more memorable for the location and was in part about supporting a cinema that has lasted the test of time.

'Well, that was charming, but if I was local, I'd definitely bring a cushion,' was Mrs Fuller's verdict.

It brought to mind the county cricket fans that come prepared for a day at Headingley or Scarborough with their Yorkshire County Cricket Club padded cushion.

As we walked back to our B&B, I made a mental note to find a chiropractor to fix a sudden, mystery back spasm. It was an opportunity to reflect on Scarborough's appeal. If all you do is traipse to the cricket and then home, you're missing out. It had been a day where we'd stepped back in time and the town had already won us over.

Please be patient during the cricket

Sunday breakfast is a treat as tea and coffee is ferried out by John, then Gillian pokes her head out of the kitchen to say hello. Having someone else cook you breakfast, even when you've paid for the privilege, is something I never take for granted.

There is more fresh fruit on offer than any bed and breakfast I can recall and, unusually for us, we're the first guests down. Sated for a hard day of watching cricket, it's not far to North Marine Road and there's a spring in the step.

Play starts at 11am with the gates open at 10am, or earlier for Yorkshire members, who get the perk of bagging their favoured spot in the ground. One friend described it as a miraculous event, akin to visiting Lourdes. Walking sticks are cast aside and aching limbs forgotten in the rush to secure a prime viewing location.

The forecast is for rain in the hour before the cricket commences. This ominous prediction and the prospect of a delayed start has thinned the flock of early birds at the main gate. In fact, the queue is more of a polite huddle.

There are separate turnstiles for OAPs and members which, if I'm being honest, is a little confusing. Today, there's no heaving migration, though it is remarkable how many materialise from nowhere as the shutters judder into life.

Quick off the blocks is a gentleman with bushy eyebrows and a tawny coloured fleece, who fairly flies through the gates and weaves his way through the pace-setters to lead the pack and get to the prize of pavilion seating in first position. Placing a coat or a bag on the white plastic seat is enough to secure it for the duration and it beats peeing round the base of your seat as an act of marking territory.

Just inside are a pair of men in blue 'Yorkie' T-shirts identifying them as volunteer helpers from the Yorkshire Cricket Foundation. The charity launched the Yorkies initiative in 2015 for the England vs New Zealand Test match and its popularity meant the match day support has been retained for internationals and county games.

It's Mick's first Festival and he sounds like a newspaper seller as the cry of 'Scorecards! Scorecards! Get yer scorecards!' rings out.

With time to spare, the tea room is calling me. I head over to browse through the donated cricket books now housed in a bookcase by the door. Titles of the ilk of *Hit for Six, Cricket My Happiness* and *Spinning round the World* encourage closer inspection. Thumbing through Bernard Hollowood's 1970 green hardback *Cricket on the Brain*, I strike up a conversation with the man next to me.

Not for the first time during the Festival does someone

eye me up and down, lost in thought.

'I know you from somewhere.'

'Oh, really? Sounds ominous.'

I bite my tongue. Just behind him, there is my poster in the tea shop window with quite a large photo of me looking vaguely respectable. Amazing what an ironed shirt can do, but he hasn't spotted it.

'You're John Fuller, aren't you? I thought I recognised you.'

Admitting that I am is always a little bit of a gamble. To my surprise, being recognised as a cricket writer happens more than you'd think in Yorkshire. It's usually on a cricket club field somewhere and there is a millisecond where I have to assess if the person's demeanour suggests he or she merely want to talk amicably about some aspect of the recreational game. Option B is that one of my grumpy tweets has struck a nerve and a lengthy, ill-tempered debate is on the tip of the tongue.

Malcolm is no such hardship. It turns out we've already swapped emails about the Scarborough Cricket Festival and, in fact, he bought my first book and left it on a train to Newcastle so others might have a read too. I think it was by accident, but either way, I like the idea of our rail network as reading shuttle runs, spreading books around the region as mobile libraries.

He recalls the 1970 Fenner Trophy Final, where Yorkshire lost to Hampshire that saw a hundred each for Geoffrey Boycott and Barry Richards. Malcolm's memory is of Richards apparently coming out to bat in plimsolls.

Malcolm is full of anecdotes, such as sitting in the deckchairs by the marquee in 1983 when Brian Johnston was President of Scarborough Cricket Club and seeing him dance at the lunch interval with his daughter as the band played.

A tradition long since lost, the band used to be in full swing during the cricket itself and everyone would stand to attention for the national anthem at the end of the day, which had been known to catch cricketers unawares.

There was also the time when the South African Fezelas took on Yorkshire Second XI over two days in July of 1961.

Umpire John Hampshire told Malcolm about a ball throwing contest that took place during the match where Hampshire managed a useful effort from in front of the pavilion, one bounce, to hit the Trafalgar Square seats on the other side of the ground. Colin Bland, who was to become known as an outstanding fielder of his generation, sent a rocket throw unerringly into the same stands without bouncing.

As it happens, Yorkshire's Director of Cricket Martyn Moxon remembers the ferocity of John Hampshire's throwing arm too. Moxon mentioned to me that he would go to the Festival as a young kid with his grandparents and was struck by how Hampshire, in the slips, would hurl it like a rocket, underarm, to Geoffrey Boycott at mid-off to sting his hands. You sometimes see the same antics today, when players try to catch specific fielders out as the ball makes its way back to the bowler.

Meanwhile, perhaps my favourite tale of Malcolm's concerns his mum regaling of a family holiday to Scarborough in 1948 and staying in a bed and breakfast in Trafalgar Square. His parents' bedroom overlooked the ground and his brother would sit by the window, entranced by Bradman's 1948 Australians, only moving during lunch and tea intervals.

My first conversation with a cricket fan at the Festival proved to be as fruitful as I'd imagined, but there was more to come from the dyed-in-the-wool devotee. 'Cricket is Life,' is his battlecry, thumping his chest, when asked what makes Scarborough so important.

He sheepishly admits to feeling melancholy if circumstance forces an absence from a county game at the coast, as was the case with the Surrey fixture. Such unpalatable inconveniences force a grimace and I suspect he's not alone there.

It turns out Malcolm is an avid cricket book collector and has thousands in his collection. Mrs Malcolm is less chuffed with being up to her eyeballs in publications with several rooms now full to the brim.

'A've had to sneak 'em in t'house from t'boot o' t'car without t'wife spotting me.'

You can imagine Wisden Almanacks, their yellow covers glowing like street lamps, stuffed under armpits and snuck into the residence at the dead of night.

* * *

With the ground filling up, I make my way to the press box for the start of the morning session. On the walk along the boundary seats by the Popular Bank, both Yorkshire and Worcestershire coaches are hitting high catches to cricketers stationed on the boundary, as supporters watch.

It strikes me as a tad dangerous, but no-one is clonked as Andrew Gale sends cricket balls up into the heavens, with Jack Brooks and Matthew Fisher looking as if they are shelling peas in their sleep.

One of the Yorkshire contingent, I think it's new signing Josh Poysden, is wearing crisp white fielding gloves; a rarity in itself and they strike an odd sight. Part professional sportsman, part magician or butler.

A teenager watches this demonstration keenly from her station on the front row; enveloped in a blue fluffy blanket that appears to be only partially offsetting the morning chill.

Yorkshire's captain Steve Patterson is by the gap between pavilion and the wooden seats, in conversation with a fan, voicing his frustration at the injury to his left ring finger that is strapped and loose by his side.

Children from the Yorkshire Cricket Foundation's beach cricket tournament are wrestling with a sizeable Yorkshire flag and being instructed in how to display it. There's a pink companion of sponsor and tourist organisation, Welcome to Yorkshire. After some shuffling, the flags are lined up so umpires and players can take the field through this floating sea of material.

At the North Stand, I duck into the tunnel with the

whitewashed walls, past the sign identifying 'Press and Scorers only' and glance at the infamous 'Hopps Inn' toilet, as chronicled in a previous chapter. To the uninitiated, the steep stairs could be winding up to a dusty attic. The creaky door spits you out into the press box where John Potter, Yorkshire's scorer, is stationed in the far right corner and half blinks, half waves a hello.

Chris Waters, *Yorkshire Post* cricket correspondent, is on the edge of the elevated back row and I squeeze by to plonk next to my good friend and veritable encyclopaedia David Warner. I rummage in my black rucksack for a device that is to prove a lifesaver over the course of the Festival.

It cannot just be my smartphone whose battery dwindles at breathtaking speed, throwing up its arms in exasperation before giving up the ghost entirely in less than a day. My tubular mobile battery pack would revive a flagging phone's fortunes and ensure nothing was missed due to electronic misfortune.

When I bought it online, I envisaged a sleek lump of shimmering tech, a nugget of gold that would catch the eye and solve any unforeseen energy consumption issues. When it arrived in the post, it was quite clearly a heavy, sparkly pink lipstick with a USB port at one end.

Outside, there's a bit of faffing as the pre-match proceedings ramp up, including what a press release assures us is the world's largest Yorkshire flag, and obligatory pink pom-poms. I'm no keen follower of vexillology, but I was a little underwhelmed by the 50-

square-metre flag. It sounds big until you put it in a cricket field.

* * *

Pleasantries done with, play gets underway and Yorkshire's Harry Brook is the first wicket of the 2018 Scarborough Cricket Festival when he is dismissed for six, pulling a delivery off Josh Tongue to deep square-leg. He drags himself off, rehearsing where the ball was meant to go, while I ponder a headline about pulling a tongue.

So far, so true to form in the sense that the North Marine Road pitch is offering pace and bounce, despite overnight rain. It's just inside the first hour when Adam Lyth also has to make his way back after overbalancing and being trapped lbw by Ed Barnard.

Up here in the Gods, a prime viewing spot behind the bowler's arm, it's possible to watch the stands come to life as spectators filter in. The forecast has been more pessimistic than the weather we've actually had, but only the West Stand is a little sparse.

You could write your own book about the science – or lack thereof – relating to how and when a cricket ball chooses to swing. Suffice it to say that as we nudge towards the lunch interval, Worcestershire begin to get the ball to hoop. It lifts the visitors who scent further wickets and their strangled lbw shouts are met with the commonplace retort heard at Headingley or Scarborough:

'Give over.'

'Quit beggin'!'

'Gerron wi' it.'

Or, if you're particularly lucky, a combination of all three. It belies a nervousness that proves to be prophetic as Yorkshire slip to 78-4 at lunch with Gary Ballance and Tom Kohler-Cadmore both caught at close quarters by the fielder at point.

Kohler-Cadmore's dad, Mick, is on Yorkshire's staff and has the benefit of TV replays. At the end of the day, he relayed the news to me that his son missed it as the ball thudded into Tom's shoulder and left a scarlet bruise. Not out after all. Such are the fine margins; many of which public and media aren't privy to.

When Yorkshire's duo of Kane Williamson and Jonny Tattersall walked out to rebuild the innings, it was time to pop out of the ground and grab some lunch at our old faithful, the North Bay Cafe on the corner.

In a new development, a yellow sign has been stuck up above the counter that nearly pokes me in the eye. It states matter-of-factly: 'Please be patient during the cricket' – a prerequisite for Yorkshire fans at the minute, but actually in relation to the prospect of orders stacking up.

* * *

Back at the cricket, the afternoon session on the first day sees Yorkshire knuckle down. Kane Williamson looks unfussy and unflustered. The best Test batsmen in the world appear to reinvent time, turning fearsome rockets into floating beach balls.

I sit in a deckchair next to Scarborough Cricket Club's groundsman John Dodds. As with most groundsmen, the art of grassmanship came later in life to Dodds, who trained as a motor mechanic when he left school. After a decade in oil-coated overalls, the building trade came next at a company that refurbished bus garages.

Alongside work, John was a club cricketer at Stamford Bridge Cricket Club. That led onto groundsmanship, as he took over the reins maintaining the ground at Low Catton Road in the village.

Fifteen years at Stamford Bridge taught Dodds plenty. He set up his own business assisting cricket clubs with their squares and went on to prepare pitches for Yorkshire Seconds as Stamford Bridge became a regular county outground.

John's burgeoning reputation as a groundsman meant he was nudged by the Durham Coach Geoff Cook to take on a full-time role at South Northumberland Cricket Club when they were recruiting for ground staff. The club, located in the Gosforth area of Newcastle, wanted someone to improve the facility to a level where they could host county cricket.

Ambitions matched and Dodds spent five years there taking it to where he thought it could go. He was then asked to become the groundsman at Scarborough. He couldn't refuse: 'How can I turn this job down? It's gone full cycle.'

One of John's favourite memories was the epic Festival encounter of 2015 between Yorkshire and Durham when

25 wickets had fallen in little over a day. Yorkshire were 79-5 in their second innings and a nip-and-tuck affair seemed set with low scores and a question of who would blink first.

I remember it clearly too. Glenn Maxwell was met in the middle by Adil Rashid just before lunch. Rashid blazed at a few needlessly that got the Yorkshire members into a lather. I opted to take a stroll around Scarborough and missed much of a record sixth-wicket partnership against Durham as Maxwell (140) and Rashid (127) hit it everywhere.

John and I get to discussing how North Marine Road has changed over the years. Once known for being a bang-to-rights draw because of a dead pitch, it turned that unwelcome status around before John's time:

'I do encourage bounce, I've always had a knack wherever I've been. The groundsman who taught me a lot, Mike Corley (Scarborough Groundsman from 1984), always said I knew exactly when to get on and when to get off a roller. That's the single, biggest secret.'

It's all about the rolling, apparently. Too much and you can flatten the demons, which is why experiments with the use of a heavy roller in county cricket draw lively debate; the captain of the batting side making a gesture to request a ten-tonne articulated lorry to drive up and down.

Dodds remembers a year when the heavy roller was allowed at will. Andrew Gale cashed in with the bat and John credits that partially down to the pitch being killed, legitimately it ought to be noted, with the opposition unable to buy a wicket.

Similarly, rolling pitches when they are dry is a recipe for disaster. He nods towards the cricket where the crowd are warming their hands with applause for a crisp Jonny Tattersall boundary.

'If I was to get on a roller out there, I could spend 15 minutes and you wouldn't get a wicket.'

I resist the temptation to suggest some guerilla rolling overnight might reawaken Yorkshire's cause.

In fact, before Dodds' tenure, the Scarborough pitch was rated as 'poor' in 2000 and Yorkshire were penalised eight points. An ECB pitch panel decided that the pitch offered undue seam movement and irregular bounce because of the amount of grass left on.

There's none of that nowadays, but there's a constant assessment and recalibration for a county groundsman. Dodds admits that he was second-guessing himself after the opening session of this current Festival game (when Yorkshire's four wickets fell quickly) but was eventually content that the wickets were not as a result of his intervention.

He sees his role as custodian of an arena for entertainment. Yes, striving for an even contest between bat and ball, but conscious that a groundsman has a responsibility to prepare wickets that get fans gripped.

John's critical of pitches around the country that are slow and dead, smiling as he tells me of a group of MCC members who now come every year and became members at Scarborough because of the setting and as the cricket's rarely dull.

Of course, drama out in the middle can be misconstrued as the fault of the groundsman. A few hours into the Festival, Dodds already had a gentleman stride out purposefully at lunch to confront him over the greenness of the pitch and the way it was cut.

John takes it all in his stride and shrugs off the barbs hurled in his direction. If there's a big hundred then he's been told before by fans he should be sacked and if wickets tumble, it must be the fault of those precious 22 yards.

Well, he must be doing something right given the stack of awards that have racked up, winning Outground of the Year four times in five years.

Scarborough's ground has hosted international men's cricket twice down the years, with England playing West Indies on August 26, 1976, with Viv Richards unfurling a match-winning hundred. Two years later, England won by 19 runs against New Zealand when the class of '78, led by Graham Gooch's 94, prevailed over Mark Burgess's side.

In John Dodds' time at the club, England Women have twice played India here in the ICC Women's Championship of 2014, but it is his involvement in other countries that also brings back memories.

He went out to assist in the preparation of the pitch for Kenya's World Cup match against South Africa at Amstelveen, May 26, 1999, where the stadium had been built in an area of a huge swathe of hockey pitches.

John also travelled to Toronto when Canada hosted the 2001 ICC Trophy (the qualifying tournament for the 2003

World Cup) and prepared pitches all over the region. It was a frenetic time for groundsmen involved as the enlarged tournament featured 22 teams, from Uganda to Nepal and Bermuda to Fiji.

He laughs fondly about his time at Maple Leaf Cricket Club, about half an hour north of the city, where Dodds' support was the 77-year-old resident groundsman and two Chinese helpers who didn't speak a word of English.

Thoughts turn back to Scarborough and I'm curious to what extent John has directions from Yorkshire County Cricket Club on types of pitches to prepare, but he insists that the club lets him get on with it. The only request he had from Jason Gillespie during the Australian's tenure was: 'All I will ever ask from you is that the nicks carry to slip.'

We sit in the Scarborough sunshine and watch as Kane Williamson chops the ball onto his stumps off Moeen Ali for 87 and a sigh reverberates around. Yorkshire are midway through pressing the self-destruct button. From 151-5, they slip to 155-8, as Willey and Bresnan go cheaply.

Amid this rollercoaster, John shares his view on groundsmanship. He sees ground staff as cogs in shaping the careers of future county cricketers and internationals and is no advocate of doctoring pitches to make them spin or seam excessively. He'd like county groundsmen to be employed by the ECB to take any impartiality out of the equation, made trickier for outgrounds given they only get a few county games.

Our attention is distracted by Yorkshire's Jack Brooks

who's just planted a six into the crowd. There are raucous cheers at the entrance gate as a portly bloke clutching a pint has the dilemma of whether to go for the catch or conserve his beer. The latter wins out.

Throughout the Festival, I hear fans bemoan the lack of characters in county cricket and the absence of interaction with the crowd. Nonetheless, Brooks is certainly an entertainer and his breezy knock of 38 is the cornerstone of a partnership of 56 with Matthew Fisher before Yorkshire succumb to 216 all out.

John gets up to marshal his troops and I take a stroll. The tea interval is the signal for hundreds to fill the outfield in a matter of minutes. Some eye John's handiwork as his team inspect and sweep the wicket; others take the shortest route to the tea room or bowl their devilish leg-spin as close catchers hunch attentively around the bat.

I like walking out to the middle and slowly taking in the full 360-degree panorama, to get the perspective of all the players who have added North Marine Road to their CVs down the years. While my playing days are now behind me, like many on the outfield now, this is as close as I've ever got to joining the professional ranks, which makes it no less a moment to savour.

* * *

I was curious about Jason Gillespie's thoughts on Scarborough and an interview came after the Festival, the day after the extraordinary Essex win by one wicket over

Surrey that concluded the County Championship season. Champions Surrey were aiming to finish unbeaten. They conceded a 410-run first innings lead at the Kia Oval, but almost broke a world record with their run chase.

Sussex, where Jason is head coach, had been defeated by six wickets inside two days at the hands of Northamptonshire to round off an otherwise encouraging season where they finished third in Division Two of the County Championship and made the final of the T20 Vitality Blast.

In a snapshot of the life of a sought-after professional cricket coach, Gillespie's about to dash for a Sussex board meeting and is busy packing up his flat before flying back to Australia for winter. Having led the Adelaide Strikers to the Big Bash League title in February 2018, he's gearing up for another hectic season back home.

There's no off-season nowadays for international cricketers – or coaches like Gillespie – who choose to swap between Northern and Southern Hemispheres and smash through time zones. It was while still at Yorkshire County Cricket Club that he agreed to coach the Adelaide Strikers during the English winter in a sign of the times. No more are coaches necessarily tied to a county all year round.

Jason Gillespie's playing résumé needs little introduction, but when did that ever stop me? Other than 259 Test wickets for Australia and the batting landmark of 201 not out against Bangladesh, the fast bowler ended his career with 613 first-class wickets.

He was signed for Yorkshire for 2006 and 2007,

claiming 59 first-class wickets and among a blizzard of stats, my eye was drawn to 123 not out against Surrey, batting at 10, which is notable as he shared a whopping, ninth-wicket stand of 246 with Tim Bresnan.

Gillespie's first match at Scarborough was the July 2006 encounter with Warwickshire in the Liverpool Victoria County Championship and it merits a brief mention.

The home side's innings and 96-run victory saw the Australian snap up five wickets in the match, but it was also Adil Rashid's first-class debut for Yorkshire that yielded 6-67 in the second innings and Andrew Gale made his debut first-class hundred.

'Dizzy' has witnessed some mighty knocks at Scarborough. In 2007, Kent were the visitors at the end of July and Younis Khan walloped 217 not out in a drawn game. Gillespie's only Festival game was actually against Yorkshire for Glamorgan in 2008. It ended in defeat for the visitors by 49 runs, courtesy of the rain then the Duckworth-Lewis calculation.

Gillespie's impact at Yorkshire though is unquestionably as a dynamic coach. Under his tutelage, the county was promoted from Division Two in 2012, won back-to-back County Championships and also had second and third-place finishes in an eventful five-year stint.

As the 2014 County Championship title race ramped up, Yorkshire hosted Sussex at Scarborough, aiming to protect their slender lead over Nottinghamshire, with Warwickshire back in third. I was curious if there was any sense of increased expectancy and pressure now that an elusive title, missed for over a decade, was palpably close?

'A lot of people speak about 'must-win' – if you just focus on the task at hand and the right things, everything else takes care of itself. We knew that if we focussed on getting all our skills right and playing well, the scoreboard would look after itself and therefore the points table.'

He went on to elaborate on how important that pared-back approach was: 'We put a real emphasis on controlling what we could – we genuinely kept it as simple as that. As with both Championship years, we had that mindset and attitude. There wasn't any added pressure. Pressure's imagined, anyway.'

I get the sense that Gillespie keeps things uber-simple, enforcing a bubble around his squad that must have been creaking as the prospect of Yorkshire's first County Championship since 2001 edged closer.

The Rashid-Maxwell 211-run coalition on August 8, 2015, against Durham crops up. Yorkshire were 79-5, with a lead of 85 in their second innings, and everyone was seeing this contest as a low-scoring thriller until a crazy couple of hours tore up the script. Jason had a front row seat in the pavilion.

'It changed the whole game. They both got magnificent hundreds and some of the best batting I've seen in county cricket was in that partnership. It's a real vivid memory as we were in a spot of bother. We never gave up. I knew that this team had a bit about them and it was great to see.'

Jason's affinity with Scarborough, both the town and the cricket club, comes across loud and clear. I can hear the smile in his voice as he describes savouring the routine of walking the mile or so to and from the ground.

'It's certainly something that I've missed since I left Yorkshire. I miss a lot of things about Yorkshire and everyone really looked forward to the trip to Scarborough. It was the highlight of the season.'

This appreciation for Scarborough may be more nuanced, but from a coaching perspective, what matters out in the middle is where judgement lies. On that front, the North Marine Road deck got a thumbs-up, not least for its pace:

'I think it's one of the best surfaces in the whole of England because there's something in it for everyone. It moves around a little bit early with the new ball; there's always bounce and carry. The surface settles down and becomes very good for batting; bowlers can't afford to miss their lines and lengths. Later in the game, it starts to take a little bit of turn and the bounce helps spinners as well.'

What strikes me again, as we talk, is that cricket at Scarborough matters. It amazes me how often someone is able to recount a day of a match from decades past, as if retrieving a dusty book from a shelf. Given the amount of cricket played, you'd be forgiven for thinking it all merges into one. That it doesn't can only be because of the warmth for Scarborough Cricket Club and the moments that speak of outstanding cricket, friendships rekindled or family holidays past.

* * *

Back at this year's Festival, there's an unveiling at the Peasholm Park end as Scarborough have named their two commentary boxes 'Cally 1' and 'Cally 2' with a sign honouring 'Dave Callaghan, 1955-2018, The Voice of Yorkshire Cricket.'

It is a measure of Cally, the popular BBC cricket commentator who passed away in 2018 at the age of 63, that so many of us associate our summer game with his softly spoken voice welcoming us over the airwaves. This is particularly so at Scarborough, a ground he had affection for and skilfully brought to life for thousands of listeners from around the world.

There's not enough room to swing even a particularly small feline in the commentary boxes here and, as a consequence, temperature is often an issue. Windows would be opened and that in turn brought the sound of the seagulls and supporters as a companion soundtrack to Cally.

There's an art to cricket commentary that goes beyond an understanding of the perils of silly point or knowing Adam Lyth's batting average to three decimal places. To my mind, it begins and ends with the voice itself. Cally felt like he was talking to you and you alone. His intonation reassured whatever the state of play; itself no mean feat in the cauldron that is Yorkshire County Cricket Club.

His impartiality was always there and he could be counted on to lend balance, however tempestuous the cricket had been, with an astute reading of the state of play.

His was a particularly charming and well-matched symphony for county cricket at Scarborough. I spent many Festivals in his company as the BBC commentary filled my office some 90 miles away in West Yorkshire.

Cally would complete a stint on the mic and then retire to the back of the box to do his hourly cricket reports for the likes of BBC Radio York or Sheffield. At the stroke of lunch, the mic would still be on and you could hear him nattering on the phone, humming to himself or filing another report.

Off the field, a gentle, kind bloke who was knowledgeable and supportive of Yorkshire cricket, Dave worked his socks off as a master of ceremonies for every cricket event you would care to name. He struck up a strong friendship with Jason Gillespie and the two toured the cricket clubs together doing fundraising evenings as the 'Dizzy and Dave' duo.

Gillespie remembers many evenings with Cally in Scarborough. The duo would head to a quiet bar near the team hotel called Soba to dissect the day's play and put the world to rights. For a broadcaster who worked like a Trojan, the simple pleasures that Scarborough held were not to be missed. Gillespie recalls: 'I know Cally would sneak down to the seafront for fish and chips.'

The Dickie Bird Foundation quiz at the Cask Inn, where Cally oversaw the mic on the night, was always a popular social during the week.

'There'd be Yorkie supporters in the crowd. I was a bit cheeky. If there was the odd question that I didn't know an answer to, I'd see people in the crowd waving at me, trying to give me tips on what the answer was. Cally could see it, but he was trying not to be biased towards Yorkshire! It was really funny.'

I last saw Dave at the Yorkshire County age group cricket presentation evening in the Long Room at the Emerald Headingley Stadium one dark November evening in 2017. The role of a public speaker, being the glue that binds an event together with professionalism and humour, is not for everyone, but Cally always took it in his stride.

There were jokes to get the audience of parents and young cricketers chuckling. We were at the same table and got talking about this very book and his love of the Festival. As sharp as ever, Cally shared the time the Scarborough tannoy system picked up the local funeral service and was full of laughs as he described it.

It was the visit of Nottinghamshire in the 2009 LV= County Championship and as Mark Wagh walked out to bat for the visitors, The Lord is my Shepherd prayer ominously boomed out, followed by a hymn.

This time, during the 2018 Festival, the tannoy behaved itself and spectators were invited to cast their eyes in the direction of the press box for the plaque unveiling. It was a fitting gesture that his name will live on at Scarborough, a ground that is synonymous with Cally.

View from the press box

The stairs up to the press box at Scarborough remind me of heading off to hunt out old photo albums in a loft, and they creak as much as my knees. Suddenly, you're in an oblong, glass-fronted room that can feel oppressively hot and claustrophobic even with just a couple of journalists present.

Years ago, my first experience at North Marine Road was not a happy one. Having started my own cricket website, *CricketYorkshire.com*, I decided to write a feature on the Festival and opted to spend the morning of the County Championship game among the world's media up in the Gods.

Entering the press box as an unknown writer was to have quizzical or questioning glances thrown in your direction. It is a sacred space and naturally, those that cover county cricket know each other well, so the presence of strangers can cause consternation.

After all, it's a place for work rather than just a convenient vantage point to watch an hour while shooting the breeze with those who have 500 words to conjure up in the next ten minutes with a flagging laptop battery.

It's also not beyond the realm of possibility that cricket

fans filter up to the press box for a look around and a natter that has been known to drive certain journalists to distraction and who can blame them? Yes, cricket writing is not ten hours down a mine shaft with a pickaxe, but it comes with its pressures, hassles and challenges all the same.

When I poked my head into that room for the first time, I had already decided to balls it out. In fairness to those assembled that day, I could have been a second-hand car salesman who had blagged his way in out of curiosity.

In behavioural terms, a press box is an office that happens to be in a cricket ground. Routines are well worn as to where journalists sit and how they set up their kit. From Wi-Fi passwords to plugging in cables for phone chargers, we all like things to be a certain way.

Rather than cow at the back in a corner and strike up a tentative conversation, I opted to sit right at the front on my own, without speaking to anyone, as eyeballs bored into the back of my head. In retrospect, it was not the smartest move I've ever made. An uncomfortable hour passed at which point I fled to the conviviality of the wooden benches outside.

I learnt a few things that day. I would have to earn the trust of my fellow journalists, as I would be writing about Yorkshire cricket for years to come, and I was ok with that. No-one had heard of *Cricket Yorkshire* back then and I guess people want to see if you're serious and going to stick around.

Lesson number two was that, on account of it getting

hotter than the Sahara in Scarborough's press box, I would be spending as little time in there as possible. As a feature writer rather than a news reporter, I had the luxury of being able to pick my subject, timing and angle so an hour shamelessly earwigging on conversations by the front gate was always going to be as profitable as sitting in a confined space like a lab experiment, sweating prolifically.

The singular advantage to being a freelance journalist not filing daily reports is the freedom that brings, and while many writers had made Scarborough's press box their temporary home, I wasn't destined to join them. The irony is not lost on me naming a chapter 'View from the Press Box' when I've been in there half a dozen times, so I'll let others paint a picture for you.

* * *

While being in the press box doesn't guarantee you'll spot a particular moment in a game, it helps if you're present.

ESPNcricinfo Editor David Hopps remembers being at the 1986 Scarborough Cricket Festival match, specifically D.B. Close XI vs New Zealand, where Ken Rutherford hit 317 in what was the fastest triple-century (234 balls) in first-class history. It had eclipsed Viv Richards' knock against Warwickshire the year before.

Asda sponsored the Scarborough Cricket Festival back then and the assembled press would be royally treated, with beer and wine flowing at lunchtime in the marquee. It was a rare occasion where Hopps would allow a tipple while on duty:

'That day we lurched out into the bright sunlight at about ten past three. We missed the first hour of the afternoon session to find out Rutherford had already gone past a hundred and we hadn't seen a ball of it! This famous incident in Scarborough Cricket Festival history, I was there, but I didn't see any of it.'

I tracked down Ken Rutherford over in New Zealand, now CEO of Waikato Racing Club in Hamilton, to ask for his memories of what remains the highest one-day knock of all-time at Scarborough. In an era before sports science, nutrition and analysts, his pre-match preparation for that stellar triple hundred was centred around many pints of bitter as Yorkshire's Willie Watson was toasting his birthday with a Scarborough pub crawl.

As Rutherford explains, that monster innings was definitely not one borne from a long lie-in. 'One of my (largely infantile) social rules while on a cricket tour was that as long as the captain was out socialising, it was OK for the 'rank-and-file' to stay out. As Jeremy Coney was last seen in the house bar of our hotel lighting Galianos at 4am, I thought it OK to have my one-for-the-road.'

Later the same day with the prospect of cricket drawing near, Ken's warm-up was apparently no more arduous than a cup of tea and a biscuit.

'I recall Bruce Edgar having the lack of grace to be dismissed very early on Day Two and my being thrust into the Scarborough sunshine. I nicked my first or second ball from Rod Estwick just short of Geoff Boycott at first slip and must confess I had hoped it might have carried. I was feeling fairly ordinary. The next ball was whacked through the covers for four and things took off from there.'

Rutherford had some insight into how the Scarborough pitch played, as he had batted there in the 1985 season in the Yorkshire League for Hull. As to what the bowling was like during his 317, tongue is partly in cheek.

'The bowling attack was a mix of the current and the old. Rod Estwick and Franklyn Stephenson were in their prime and obviously talented bowlers with proper pace. It's fair to say the balance of the attack may have been more at home in their armchair, with pipe and newspaper.'

As the carnage continued, the air of incredulity grew as the scorers struggled to keep up. The Rutherford mindset that day began with the goal of getting a hundred before lunch; not something you hear very often and as it unfolded, he couldn't quite believe it was happening. He wasn't the only one.

'The funniest moment was walking into the changing room at tea on 301 not out. Coney had slept through the whole middle session and the applause as I entered the room woke him up. He looked up at me and noted, 'Gee Ruds, are you still batting? You must be on 170 by now?'

On being told, the skipper apparently laughed at the notion that Rutherford had actually reached 300 and so team-mate John Wright recommended a look in the scorebook. Cue a jaw on the floor.

Batting records capture the headlines, but there's always the context of a partnership. Someone at the other end needs to rotate the strike and be comfortable out of the limelight. On this particularly scintillating day of cricket, that support came from all-rounder Evan Gray, who hit 88 and acted as the perfect foil. Though the result was a draw, with 102 from Javed Miandad in response, the New Zealanders' total was 519-7 declared off 94 overs, an extraordinary feat that stands up to any professional figure you'll see in a single day.

* * *

A media colleague who has spent many days at North Marine Road is Chris Waters, the current Cricket Correspondent at the *Yorkshire Post*, who watched his first county game at Scarborough in July 1988. It was the 40-over Refuge Assurance League between Yorkshire and Lancashire, and Waters, in his teens, recalls winning permission to go and watch live cricket:

'Up on a family holiday from Lincoln and staying for a week in Whitby, I persuaded my parents to take me over to Scarborough on the bus. They went off to the Sea Life Centre with my brother and I went to the match on my own and sat in the Trafalgar Square End. It made a real impression on me; the ground and the surroundings. It was a nondescript game, but it was a big moment for me. I'd never seen an inter-county match before.'

In that game, Yorkshire scored 208-8 off their 40 overs as Ashley Metcalfe top-scored with 69. Lancashire's bowling attack certainly had variety with Ian Austin shuffling in to bowl his efficient yorkers and Wasim Akram's boomeranging pace dismantling the laws of physics.

The visitors snuck home by two wickets and would go on to claim third place behind Champions Worcestershire with Yorkshire languishing in mid-table. Back then, it was every county lumped in together playing 16 games. On the surface, a marathon with many games on which nothing particularly hinged. Yet, had I pored over my revision at school with the same forensic focus as the County Championship table, who knows where I'd be now?

Chris's first memory of Scarborough as a journalist came when he visited Yorkshire to cover Nottinghamshire in the 2001 edition of the Norwich Union League, a few days after Yorkshire had won the County Championship.

'There was a carnival atmosphere at the ground. I was working for the *Nottingham Evening Post* and it was the famous match when Darren Lehmann got 191 off 103 balls, which remains the most dramatic innings I've ever seen.'

Many of you, certainly of a Yorkshire persuasion, will remember it. Yorkshire Phoenix beat Nottinghamshire Outlaws by 179 runs and more than 6,000 cheered themselves hoarse as the Australian left-hander hit the highest one-day innings for the county and Yorkshire's 352-6 was a record one-day total.

Chris got stuck on the A64 and might never have seen the landmark knock. 'It was Bank Holiday Monday and gridlocked. I seriously thought about turning round and going back. I got to the ground late and walked into the

Yorkshire press box, thick with cigarette smoke and pipes in the old days. I remember 'Plum' (David Warner) was kind to me and found me a spot.'

Inevitably, these batting records get broken and, at the time of writing, Yorkshire's 411-6 against Devon down at Exmouth in 2004 will take some beating. Back then, an individual innings of 191 was the kind of punishing show of strength and concentration that few were capable of. Yorkshire fell to 52-2 and then the fun started as Lehmann got to work with his 11 sixes.

Waters has seen more than his fair share of county cricket, but even so, it was more than just a mathematical landmark.

'It was really unusual at the time. Nowadays, this kind of striking is more common, but then it was really rare. It felt that you were witnessing something quite sensational. He just kept peppering the old wooden seats with sixes. I remember I nearly got whacked by one of them walking round to the tea bar as it thudded into the wooden hut behind me. That was nearly the end of my cricket writing career at Scarborough!'

Through all of the interviews, it's clear that cricket at Scarborough has a profound effect on people and Chris sums it up as well as any.

'It's the intimacy of the venue. Spectators can get on top of the action like a ballet looking down onto the pitch. It's the proximity to the sea, where you can take a stroll over at lunch or before play. It's such a characterful ground with the houses at the Trafalgar Square End; a bit of a throwback. It's the essence of county cricket as many people understand it and love it.'

* * *

No book about the Scarborough Cricket Festival would be complete without the Australian batting maestro Darren Lehmann. His county cricket career with Yorkshire spanned 1997 to 2006 during which time he scored 14,352 runs.

At Scarborough, he made hay, won the County Championship and broke the one-day batting record that still stands today. If you ask any Yorkshire fan, of a certain vintage, who ranks as the county's greatest overseas player, Lehmann usually heads the list. An accolade earned over a decade of service and in sharp contrast to the flitting cameos of overseas cricketers now.

Before the interview, I get to thinking about nicknames. Lehmann's is 'Boof,' given to him as a 12-year-old by a mate called Johnny Giannetto, as they played Aussie Rules football in the South Australian town of Gawler.

It was a nod to a particularly impressive bouffant hairstyle at the time, now a touch ironic given it has been replaced many years later by a bald dome. It's not inconceivable that Lehmann also made that kind of audible noise, 'Boof!' as he shipped another six out of North Marine Road.

The context to this interview is intriguing. Lehmann is currently between coaching roles, his own cricket academy notwithstanding, but is inked in for media stints with a local radio station. In the hours after we talk, a story breaks around the world about the emotional impact the aftermath of the Australian ball-tampering scandal, that cost Darren his job as Australia's national coach, still has on him.

The Longstaff review into the culture of the national governing body, Cricket Australia, has been scathing and debate is swirling about possible reductions for the player bans of ex-captain Steve Smith, vice-captain David Warner and batsman Cameron Bancroft.

Amidst all of this, Lehmann is sparing time to talk about a muscular and profitable decade of his life when he was 'boof'-ing the ball to all parts in a Yorkshire sweater. His reputation may have taken a hammering since the scandal that engulfed Australian cricket broke in March 2018, but here in Yorkshire, it remains intact and revered.

We set up timings to catch up through the online application Skype. This in itself is a bit of a mission. I spend half an hour trying to log in. Don't get me started on how Microsoft do things.

I'm sent verification codes and then codes to verify my verification codes. I want to log in to an account to do a phone interview in another country, not smash open the vaults of the Bank of England.

When all is set up, we have to connect and the routine way of doing that on Skype is give him 'a wave' using an emoticon, a facial expression to express a mood. Originally, I stood firm against the laziness of emojis – the crying yellow face being the prime example – but have since shamefully folded and joined in.

Here on Skype, I can't bring myself to 'wave' at Darren. It's a journalist-sportsman relationship, not a primary school class. So, I type out a bit of an introduction and ping off the invite. Now, it's time to fret about time zones. By my calculation, I can fit in watching a film then hop onto Skype at 11pm and it will be 9am the next day in Brisbane. Just when a plan comes together, it promptly falls apart.

Moira and I spend five minutes having an animated discussion about what day it is. We've both been under the pump running our businesses, working from home where days fudge together. You soon fall out of the regular patterns that those who commute to work tend to frame their weeks by. What day is it? It helpfully turns out to be a Wednesday.

At the appointed time, Darren calls me and there's what might kindly be called a tech fail. He can hear me and see me, but unfortunately, there's no audio for me which makes an interview tricky unless we resort to charades.

He's well-lit, sat in his office in a T-shirt. The morning has broken in Brisbane whereas, in the flickering moments where the video call worked well, I look like I'm a wild hermit living in a dark cave. I opt to call Darren back and, hey presto, it's as if he's in the next room. When it behaves, technology is a marvel, there's absolutely no lag between West Yorkshire and Queensland, although it's fortunate it isn't chucking it down as my broadband is notoriously dodgy in the rain; something of a problem in the UK.

Lehmann is quickly into his stride remembering the

holiday feel of Scarborough with crowds wedged in shoulder to shoulder and a reliable wicket for going big with the bat. The way he tells it, it felt like a basin stocked with Northern fervour: 'You're in a sort of cauldron and they're all supporting Yorkshire.'

One of the stand-out Lehmann innings at Scarborough, mentioned earlier in this chapter, took place just a few days after Yorkshire had sealed the 2001 Cricinfo Championship by beating Glamorgan at North Marine Road.

The fanfare of sealing the first County Championship since 1968 brought a party atmosphere and a bumper crowd to their Norwich Union League match against Nottinghamshire on the same ground.

Sleep-deprived after being up all night celebrating an enormous moment on the county's honours list, Lehmann picked up his cricket helmet to go out to bat and found a bubbly pick-me-up inside:

'It was a big couple of days. We didn't train or anything before that game. It was just walk-out-and-play. There was some champagne there in the helmet, I just drank that, walked out and batted. I can remember being not too stressed. After the stress of not winning a Championship for so long, there was relief on everyone's faces, so there was no pressure. I can remember saying, "Sit back and enjoy, lads," as I walked out.'

In one of the masterfully understated quotes you'll read, his summation of taking the Nottinghamshire bowlers to the cleaners was merely: 'I just got lucky. I had one of those lucky days.' This was Twenty20 carnage several years before the new format would make its debut in England.

In his orange-and-black kit with a Yorkshire Tea logo across the front, Lehmann smashed 191 off 103 balls. He managed to lose three balls during the onslaught and delight the spectators with his brakes-off, throw-the-kitchen-sink approach.

'I remember it being a really surreal day. A relaxed day, just going with the flow and not stopping, not slowing down. It was one of the all-time great wickets and a small grandstand side (Popular Bank) so it wasn't a big hit either. It became one of the highest scoring games of all-time in 40-over cricket.'

He warms to his theme on realising that he was seeing it like the proverbial football: 'When you were batting, you wanted to be on strike and have every ball. It was one of those games where everything came off.'

It crystallised Lehmann's unquenchable thirst for runs in both first-class and List A (or limited-overs) formats for Yorkshire. He had a hell of a year. To this day, no-one has scored more List A runs in a season for Yorkshire (1,177).

It's hardly surprising that Scarborough means a great deal to Lehmann given he averages 76 on the ground in the short form and only a shade less in what is usually known in Yorkshire as 'proper cricket.'

Yet, there is a family tie too. His brother-in-law is former Yorkshire team-mate Craig White, having married Craig's sister Andrea who he met in Scarborough. 'It was a really family-orientated time. Holidays, beaches were packed; the shorefront with slot machines. I'd never seen anything like it. For me, it had a really different feel about a game of cricket when you were playing there.'

His romance for Scarborough is reflected in what happened on and off the pitch. Andrea was working at Scarborough Hospital and went to the pub with her brother, Craig. Lehmann almost blew it as he was late to arrive after having a few beers with David Boon.

Life in Yorkshire was a steep learning curve with plenty of distinctions from back home. Lehmann remembered how the sight of spectators savouring cricket on the outfield really stuck with him.

'That was a really joyful memory of Scarborough, the amount of fans and kids that would go out and play during the day. That doesn't happen enough in the game anymore. It certainly doesn't happen in Australia.'

As a nod to that accessibility, Lehmann would himself make a point of chatting with fans and putting the world to rights with members, if Yorkshire were batting and he was out.

'Scarborough, in essence, is what cricket's all about. That mingling with fans, entertainment and having a good day at the cricket is exactly what there should be more of around the world.'

Of course, this isn't limited to Scarborough and current Yorkshire players might argue they do have plenty of interaction with fans. To be honest, it's hard not to at North Marine Road. Yet, the theme of a modern disconnect between supporters and professionals was to crop up quite a bit in my research. Whether or not we look back on decades gone with sepia-tinted fondness and allow that to blur the truth, I'll leave for you to ponder.

Lehmann savoured settling in at Scarborough for a week rather than the usual bombing about the country by car, racking up the fixtures and hundreds of miles on the road. 'The pressures of the first-class game disappeared when you played in the Festival. It had a really joyful feel about it. It was almost like a mid-season break where all the travelling and touring went away because you were in this beautiful, seaside town.'

While he established himself as a lynchpin for Yorkshire, winning his cap in 1997 and captaining them in 2002, Lehmann did not fulfil all of his ambitions in England. He had moved from Australian State representation to county cricket and so didn't end up playing club cricket in Yorkshire.

'It's my biggest regret actually, not playing league cricket. It would have been good to spend a year playing in the Yorkshire leagues, it's one of those things I would have loved to do.'

Just as he arrived from Australia, Lehmann recalls representing Yorkshire Academy to get a hit. It must have been quite a shock for the bowler running in, but shaking off jetlag aside, it was to be the only time.

Meanwhile, Jake, Darren's son and a first-class cricketer himself with South Australia and Yorkshire, had two stints at English clubs with Reigate Priory in Surrey and Cannock in Birmingham: 'He's loved the opportunity as a young man. I didn't do it and that was my fault really.'

It teaches a cricketer to adapt to everything from having to do your own ironing to getting to grips with fielding in England in April, with the ball zipping all over the place and the cold digging its claws in.

Afterwards, I talk about Darren's interview with Mrs Fuller and feigning an awful Australian accent, pretend to be Lehmann glugging back the champagne in his helmet.

'He met his wife in Scarborough,' I tell her.

'Is she South African too?'

Maybe I'll leave the impersonations to the professionals.

* * *

Veteran sports commentator John Helm is another for whom the Scarborough Cricket Festival has made quite an impact. He left the BBC for Yorkshire Television in 1981 and part of his remit, other than a focus on all things football, was to cover Yorkshire County Cricket Club. As it happens, that suited him rather well as cricket was John's first love.

Born in the West Yorkshire town of Baildon, he played for the club from about the age of seven and has been President of Baildon Cricket Club for nearly 40 years. Helm used to be a decent Bradford League cricketer, but advice from uncompromising Yorkshire batsman Arthur Mitchell put paid to any pretensions of representing his county.

Mitchell was famed for his blunt and brutal assessments as a coach and convinced Helm to switch from being a leg-spinner. The reasoning was that, at the time, Yorkshire wouldn't employ one. According to John, a promising trajectory subsequently fizzled out as off-spinners were two-a-penny.

Helm's connection to Yorkshire cricket is deep-rooted, right down to his neighbours.

'I was born on Maude Avenue. Four doors away on the same side of the street lived Ronnie Burnet, ex-captain of Yorkshire. Immediately opposite him was Arthur Mitchell, the coach of Yorkshire. Two doors away on the other side was a lady called Mrs Summers, Phil Sharpe's auntie.'

Helm was even taught shorthand by the sister of England spinner Jim Laker, so he really was close to cricket.

John has gone on to become synonymous with ITV football commentary, but in his BBC stint from 1975 he produced the giant of radio programmes that is Test Match Special, as well as one-day finals of the Gillette Cup.

In his debut season at the mic for Yorkshire Television (now ITV Yorkshire), Helm travelled across the outgrounds that Yorkshire still used then: Bradford Park Avenue, Middlesbrough's Acklam Park, St George's Road in Harrogate, Sheffield Collegiate's Abbeydale Park HQ and North Marine Road.

The demand to cover county cricket at Scarborough was considerable. 'I absolutely loved it. We used to almost fight off the cameramen to do the job as everybody knew the reputation of the Festival and what a good week it was.'

One year, the idea came to fit microphones to the

umpires during a Festival game, something that had never been done before. The two umpires Barrie Leadbeater and John Hampshire were the guinea pigs. In place in the commentary box, John remembers it didn't go exactly to plan:

'The first ball of the morning was tickled to fine leg by the opening batsman and he came down the wicket. One of the umpires asked him: "Did you pull that bird in the bar last night?" which was going out live! The experiment lasted about one ball.'

Helm also calls to mind a stint in the commentary box by Geoffrey Boycott who had not long since retired.

'I'll never forget he came in wearing a canary yellow suit, he got enormous stick from the crowd as he walked round. Ian Botham was batting and what we didn't know was he had a bet that he'd hit the ball into the gantry. He did! He hit this massive six straight down the ground into the commentary box. We've still got the recording of Boycott leaping out of the way, screaming, as an unexpected piece of red leather came hurtling towards him.'

While the Scarborough Cricket Festival united them that day, their paths would diverge not long after. Boycott has since become a household name in cricket commentary while John's career moved squarely over to football. In fact, as our discussion came to a close, he was about to swap a West Yorkshire winter for covering the Indian Super League.

* * *

Stuart Rayner is a sports writer and author who you may know from his successful debut book, *The War of the White Roses: Yorkshire Cricket's Civil War, 1968-1986*, analysing life and the turbulence at the county club during Boycott's era.

When we caught up, Stuart was sat in front of a box of old programmes and scorecards from Scarborough. He'd been a junior member at the Club for a few years and chose a random box from his collection to uncover annual reports and statements of accounts from 1991 and 1992.

As you'd imagine, many cricket journalists begin life as fans themselves, long before taking up the pen or keyboard. I am not a hoarder myself, but I too had scorecards and signed memorabilia. As a young lad, I would walk from school to the County Ground at Taunton to watch Somerset County Cricket Club and saw those players as idols.

Stuart is from Scarborough and the first match he went to was the Refuge Assurance League game of 1988 between Yorkshire and Lancashire that Chris Waters mentioned earlier. What are the chances? Two young cricket fans struck by the same cricket match and destined to share a press box years later.

'My mother was more of the cricket fan of my two parents. I've got two younger brothers as well and she was always of a mind that, "I'm not taking them to watch three- and four-day cricket until I know they've got the patience to do it!" I remember going along and being hugely excited.'

While Scarborough's a cricketing town and the game is part of Yorkshire's DNA from village green upwards, Rayner junior had seen Yorkshire's Benson & Hedges Cup win of 1987 the year before on telly and been primed for what was to come.

So, why the appeal of Scarborough Cricket Club? What converted him to cricket in a heartbeat? 'I think it's the intimacy of it. I'm a big football fan, but to go to top-level cricket opposed to top-level football, particularly at Scarborough, you were so close to everyone. I'd happily go off and get everyone's autographs, which I'd never do at the football.'

Stuart would sit on the Popular Bank and recalls that fluidity between much-loved players and spectators. 'I remember Graeme 'Foxy' Fowler. I saw him play a few times for Lancashire and Durham there and he'd often field on the cover boundary. Between overs, he'd go and sit on the seats and chat to the bloke in the front row!'

As an hour flits by, stories tumble out, told with affection of a time that feels like it's slipping away, if not entirely gone: 'I remember this massive queue, must have been early Nineties, snaking along the boundary to get Phil Simmons' autograph. He'd sign a couple, then the ball gets bowled, he'd sign a couple more.'

Stuart's mental picture of Peter Hartley and David Byas sat on the wooden seats having a cigarette certainly speaks to a different era for spectators. Fans playing cricket on the ground in the breaks crops up a lot as an alluring feature of Scarborough and it's what connects and captivates both

Stuart and I.

This proximity to professional cricketers dissolves that barrier between fan and pro and you never know what you'll be in a position to earwig on. Stuart recalls watching at the end of a day of Championship cricket when one of the players' mums popped up to give Michael Vaughan a lift. He was in the England Under-19 side the next day and obviously couldn't drive.

As a boy, Rayner even managed to bag the prized autograph of Geoffrey Boycott, a player he'd go on to write about at great length years later as a cricket journalist. As we swap tales from our childhoods, my own failed attempts to catch 'Beefy' back at Taunton spurs Stuart's own recollection of Botham at the Joshua Tetley Trophy Semi-Final in the 1992 Festival.

'I remember Botham hitting a six over my head that hit the washing line of one of the B&Bs behind the Popular Bank! I couldn't tell you who won the game or how many Botham scored or anything, apart from that.'

As a Scarbadian, Stuart's perspective is particularly valuable when it comes to trying to gauge how the presence of county cricket in the town is savoured and embraced (or not) by locals. As you'd expect, for those businesses offering accommodation, it's a lifeline and ties into the wider importance of tourism to the Scarborough region, the most visited holiday destination in England outside of London.

In 1992, the Pakistani fast bowlers Wasim Akram and Waqar Younis were at Scarborough but not playing, and for

Stuart, it felt that change was in the air, with touring teams no longer seeing the Festival as the relaxed final act they once had.

The drawn match was not without flair with Pakistan captain and opening bat Shoaib Mohammad striking 105 not out before he declared on 253-6 off 75 overs. Peter Sleep then replied with 182 for the World XI as Pakistan used ten bowlers.

In 2005, Stuart would return to North Marine Road in a professional capacity to relish the Festival atmosphere again, when Yorkshire welcomed Durham for a Division Two game in the Frizzell County Championship. 'Now suddenly you're sat behind the bowler's arm and the whole experience is different. You're there to work. It was very enjoyable, but a different way of doing it.'

He credits his most memorable Festival game as a journalist as being the top-of-the-table clash between Yorkshire and Durham in 2013, boasting an abundance of talent who were either playing international cricket or have since gone on to do so.

'If you speak to people from Durham now, they see that as the game that effectively won them the title. The fact that they beat Yorkshire (by seven wickets) gave them the momentum to go on and win it. Paul Collingwood still talks about it as the closest he's ever played in county cricket to a Test match.'

For the record, Durham's highest total against Yorkshire of 573 all out was off the back of hundreds from Mark Stoneman, Ben Stokes and a maiden first-class ton for

Michael Richardson. Yorkshire were nipped out for 274 with a top six boasting Phil Jaques, Kane Williamson, Jonny Bairstow and Gary Ballance. Following on, Jaques hit 152 and Williamson 97, but Durham were up to the task.

It was in this last decade where Scarborough's importance on the County Championship calendar was cemented. The crowd in that 2013 encounter between the Northern counties eclipsed the aggregate record of over 19,500 that had stood for a decade. Furthermore, it began a sequence that saw the winning team at the Scarborough Cricket Festival go on to clinch the four-day County Championship title: Durham (2013), Yorkshire (2014), Yorkshire (2015), Middlesex (2016), Essex (2017).

With rivalries split across divisions, rather than all eighteen sides playing each other as in days of old, the County Championship crackles with intrigue. Games at Scarborough have enough still riding on them.

In contrast, Stuart observed the likes of Michael Vaughan and Matthew Hoggard getting their chance at Scarborough early in their careers, as the season felt like it was winding down benevolently without the cut and thrust of promotion, relegation and title aspirations.

He can picture how county caps were often awarded at Scarborough as Rayner witnessed Vaughan receive his. In fact, it was once a brief ceremony, kept like an end-of-term prize-giving at Scarborough, to roll round again for players.

David Warner has written of the time that Gavin Hamilton and Paul Hutchison got theirs in August 1998 on the same day. Apparently, Gavin Hamilton had a week to remember with career-best figures of 6-50 and a path cleared to potentially represent England. It was at Scarborough where he received his county cap from David Byas who took off his Yorkshire sweater, passed it to Hamilton, then whipped out a cap from the umpire's pocket.

As you'd expect, 2001 crops up more than once as the year when Yorkshire won their first silverware since the 1987 Benson & Hedges Cup win over Northamptonshire. Like many fans that year, Rayner wanted to be there for the moment of history and was trying to weigh up which Scarborough fixture the County Championship could be decided at.

The Cricinfo Championship of 2001 saw Glamorgan visit North Yorkshire first in August, followed by Essex on September 12. He figured, wrongly as it turns out, that the four-day title hunt would go to the end of the season, but instead Yorkshire bagged 20 points against the Welshmen to clinch it, after a handsome victory by an innings and 112 runs.

'I missed the moment I really wanted to see because I'd just not appreciated that Yorkshire would win the title that early. I thought it would go much closer to the wire. It was still nice to see them in their title-winning season, but it was a frustration that I picked my moment so badly.'

When Stuart was born, Yorkshire hadn't won the County Championship for ten years, as he puts it: 'You thought it was never going to happen, but it was a really big deal when it did.'

He got into watching county cricket by proving his worth and attention span to his mum with limited-overs games and progressing to the longer format. While Scarborough's retention of both County Championship matches was rightly seen as a positive when the competition was slashed to 14 rounds in 2017, its loss of T20 and 50-over matches does have consequences.

In 1988, if Scarborough hadn't hosted more than four-day cricket, young Rayner wouldn't have been allowed to go and might have taken up roller disco or windsurfing instead.

With the contraction of the County Championship comes tough choices. As I write this chapter in the opulence of a Travelodge in Warwickshire listening to the lorries rumble by, I wonder how places like Scarborough will encourage their kids into county cricket without the bridge that is T20?

It's somewhat ironic that I should be worried about the lack of Twenty20 on the Yorkshire coast when there will be an entirely new form of cricket played in England from 2020 with the 100-ball format revealed to howls of derision.

While the idea of truncated T20 (minus a bit) at eight Test match grounds will be dissected long after this book has gone to print, there could yet be crumbs of comfort heading to Scarborough. To my mind, the existing T20 Blast that has won fans and seen attendances pleasingly spike will need to be played somewhere else, if it ultimately survives – so why not Scarborough and other club grounds around Yorkshire?

Expanding the offering at outgrounds allows fans of all ages to access cricket in a way that appeals most to them and could help inspire the next generation of players – and cricket writers.

Sunday evening:
Just desserts but
no Hanky Panky

Towards the end of Sunday, there are 20 overs yet to be bowled, but play is called off for the day. The abandonment has the flip side prospect of a premature meal – but not before catching up with Yorkshire first-team coach Andrew Gale.

It's been a tough few days after Yorkshire's T20 Blast defeat ramped up the pressure and now fellow County Championship strugglers Worcestershire have gained the ascendancy here at North Marine Road.

Professionalism comes in many forms. Gale is judged on results across the formats, but I imagine talking to me about his time here as a player is not front-of-mind, yet here he is.

While it might appear another lifetime ago, Scarborough was a seminal moment in Andrew Gale's career. He arrived at North Marine Road for the match against Nottinghamshire in 2013 having not hit a hundred in 33 innings. He has admitted since that he was a game or two from dropping himself, despite being captain.

'I felt under pressure for my place. I wasn't hitting the ball well and kept finding ways to get out. As a senior player and captain of the side, you want to be leading from the front, so I felt like I was letting everybody down. I had some good backing from 'Dizzy' (Jason Gillespie) and he said, "Stick at it, it will come good." I just wanted to make sure in that game at Scarborough that if I got in, I cashed in.'

The flickering flame of form is such that the game can make you feel like a superhero one minute and fumbling for a run the next. It was certainly getting to crunch-time for Yorkshire's captain and as we pick at an old wound, he talked of the need to remember the difficulties, negative headlines and past battles as motivation to go big.

His knock of 272 was 62 more runs than he'd mustered in his nine previous Championship innings. The marathon feat spanned nearly nine hours and sparked a bumper harvest with the next two visits to the crease yielding 103 against Middlesex and 148 against Surrey. For Gale, Scarborough has always been home from home, suiting his batting style and with the record to prove it, averaging 49 on the ground in first-class cricket.

In some ways, the longer the innings lasted, the more Yorkshire's skipper was able to suck in the oxygen of confidence and unlock himself from a run of low scores that had swept in self-doubt: 'There's no substitute for time in the middle. You can work as hard as you want, but if you can spend a couple of hours at the crease, suddenly, everything feels a lot better.'

Returning as coach has been nothing like the fairytale associated with that record-breaking effort back in 2013. Where once it was a Festival fortress, Scarborough is now neutral territory based on the results alone. Andrew Gale's renaissance with the bat that year wasn't actually in the Festival and Durham brought things back to earth with a bump in August as they chased 121 to register a seven-wicket win.

Since Gale took charge as first-team coach in November 2016, Yorkshire's Scarborough record reads: Loss to Somerset (179 runs), loss to Essex (8 wickets), loss to Surrey (7 wickets). He bears the same haunted look that I have when I'm trying to tackle Ikea furniture.

The parts are laid out, you think you understand both the problem and the solution, but it's just not happening:

'We try to talk about the way in which to bat here. Pitches aren't as flat as they used to be. We seem to not be getting to grips with how to score runs here. You might make mistakes once or twice, but to continually make them is disappointing.'

I threw him a bone with a question about the difficulty of switching formats so often, but he isn't having any of it. It's the same for both sides and that's no excuse. Knuckling down, leaving the ball astutely and switching the pressure back on to the bowler is the name of the game.

'You're going to get good balls here. Your name's on one at some point, but if you're willing to graft it out and get the bowlers into their third and fourth spells, it's a fast scoring ground and momentum can change quickly.'

He's deflated by the way Yorkshire had stuck at it and built a platform only to see that particular bridge collapse under them. A potential first-innings score of 300 became 216 all out after losing four wickets for just four runs. It undermined what had been shaping up nicely: 'You're thinking, "Where's that come from?" so it's immensely frustrating as coach.'

In retrospect, it was the best time to catch 'Galey' as things were about to get a whole lot worse, but we finish up with the dual-edged sword that is social media. He uses it primarily as a news feed to keep updated on what's happening around county cricket, but if there's a few big games on the schedule, he just won't look at it.

Coming into this game, Gale was well aware of what the reaction will have been and by not engaging with social media, it can't nag and niggle; he keeps his focus on the game at hand.

As it happens, he is cool-headed about a T20 victory that was swiftly overwritten by a defeat: 'Thursday night will have been "the best thing since sliced bread and all the players are brilliant," then Friday night, it will have been all my fault and "sack the coach." I know what we're trying to achieve here, we're going through transition, trying to bring in the right players and develop them at the club, but that's a bit of a bumpy ride.'

Not wanting to end on a sombre note, I ask about Gale's favourite memory at Scarborough. You'd expect 272 to be trotted out as it's not every day a batsman digs in for over a day and etches his name on the honours board. He takes a long time to think and I leave the subsequent silence unfilled. He's either mentally knackered after a long day or giving it due consideration.

Instead, it's the 183-run victory over Durham in 2015 where he didn't score any runs (12 & 1) but it was a humdinger. Durham's target was 447 and they fell well short as the reigning county champions remained unbeaten and had a lead of 53 points in the table.

For Gale as captain then, it was a crucial step towards retaining the County Championship. Winning when you're misfiring is part of the four-day journey: 'We were well below par, but moments of individual brilliance won us the game. You come off after taking the winning catch and think, "Bloody hell, we showed a lot of character there."'

* * *

I leave Yorkshire's coach to puzzle out his strategy for day two and head back to my B&B to begin the serious endeavour of deciding where to eat.

We opt for Gianni's, an Italian restaurant on Victoria Road that has the thumbs up vote from many diners on TripAdvisor, so that's good enough for us.

In order to get there, we walk down Dean Road, a horizontal traverse that cuts across the A165 and boasts an array of independent shops. A corner of a takeaway in a red brick building catches my attention. It advertises its wares proudly. Pizza. Burger. Kebab. Parmesan. Hang on! When did cheese become a headline? Who knows, maybe it's world-beating Parmesan.

Further up, there's an American candy store that's still open just before 8pm in case you have a sudden urge for peanuts, pretzels or a Hershey's bar. Next, a medium offering private readings and demonstrations of clairvoyance. It's an eclectic street.

We're fortunate to have bagged a booking at Gianni's at late notice. The restaurant is packed and there's an air of tight-lipped stress about the place.

Service is slow, but we're in absolutely no hurry and the meal itself is very good indeed. Ordering spaghetti in an Italian restaurant is either playing it safe or building up expectations unduly. This time, it was inspired. Who knew you could get that excited about meatballs?

The pudding menu brought further reward, deciding not to opt for a dessert called Hanky Panky (so public) and wisely plumping for pavlova and all of its meringue magnificence instead. There was the added advantage of being amped up with that much sugar, I was destined to finish the book by sunrise.

Monday: Letters from fans ... and roobish!

Day two at the main entrance to the cricket ground and the queue is led by a gentleman in a wide-brimmed hat who introduces himself to me as a league umpire. He couldn't make the first day as he was officiating in the Barnsley & District Cricket League, a Sunday cricket institution in South Yorkshire enjoying its 125-year anniversary in 2018.

On any given day at Scarborough, there is a melting pot of backgrounds and lives spent happily embedded in cricket. I had resolved to speak to more of the fans and was told I must sit down with David in the Members Lounge of the Pavilion.

David has been coming to the Scarborough Cricket Festival since 1964. He was unwell as a child and his family were told that a trip abroad would be restorative, but his mother decided on the fresh, salty air of Scarborough instead. An unintended consequence was the spark of a love affair with county cricket on the coast. He hasn't missed a Festival since, a sporting commitment lasting over 50 years.

He recalls swarms of greenfly causing havoc in the John

Player Special League match against Middlesex in 1979. The 40-over game was reduced to 35-overs a side as play was repeatedly interrupted and players took to covering their faces with handkerchiefs.

One of his favourite tales recalls the boom of the cannon in the naval battle performance at nearby Peasholm Park, prompting Yorkshire's Fred Trueman to fall down flat while fielding, as if hit. The mock military engagements continue to this day, but the fielders remain on their feet.

* * *

In the press box, I'm scribbling my notes from Sunday when an eerie voice jolts me back to the present. I look up startled to see if anyone else is hearing an amplified conversation over the tannoy. Sure enough, journalists pause their keyboard tapping and someone mutters, 'What the HELL is that?'

It's incredibly loud, yet hard to make out what's being said, though at one stage, a woman's laughter spookily echoes around the stadium sending chills down everyone's spines. The radio frequency for the cricket has been joined by another party, rumoured later in the day to have been BBC Look North. The only saving grace, for the host club at least, is that it's an hour before play and the interference doesn't return during the game.

It isn't the only technological snafu of the morning, with the scoreboard not showing the correct score. At one point, John Dodds comes in and checks the fuse box, but the culprit is someone who has accidentally displaced a plug with his knee, and Dodds, groundsman and one-man IT department, soon has order restored.

The morning session reveals the official attendance from yesterday as 3,450. Not too shabby, but less than I had guessed. No matter, Worcestershire progress to 104-0 with lunch approaching.

Daryl Mitchell has an 81-ball 50 and Jack Brooks dismisses Tom Fell for 45, trapping him lbw. The reaction from a bigger and livelier crowd than Sunday is more of relief than anything else. I head to the tea room for my second stint of gathering Festival stories, settling down with a brew and a notebook.

* * *

Within my earshot, conversation is turning to matters away from the county circuit. Two old boys are putting the world of league cricket to rights:

'We were at Pudsey on Saturday and they had a young umpire. He didn't give any lbws. Probably couldn't see over the top of the bloody stumps!'

A Yorkshire member, Robert, drops by to tell me of a story about his mum and Fred Trueman.

Robert was a young lad sat pitchside on the grass below the tea room while his mother sat on the wooden bench, doing some knitting during the game. Trueman was fielding on the boundary and noticed Robert's mother. He called out.

'What you knitting?'

'A jumper.'

'Would you knit me one?'

'Mr Trueman, I haven't got enough wool for you!'

Robert remembers Fred roaring with laughter as if it were yesterday.

* * *

In my research, many accounts have come to light about what cricket at Scarborough means to its fans. They're peppered throughout these pages, but this chapter collecting some of those that stood out will give a flavour of why the Scarborough Cricket Festival is so much more than the cricket itself.

Having put the call out, there was a plethora of tales to sift through. They came across on email but read like personal letters, shared with arresting honesty and crackled with emotion.

Yorkshire fan David Tindall persuaded his wife, Helen, from the other side of the Great Pennine Wall, that what she really wanted to do for a holiday was to head to Scarborough and watch the White Rose. Oh, to be a fly on the wall for those kind of conversations. They must happen up and down the county from Sheffield to Stamford Bridge and Halifax to Hull.

'Want to go to Scarborough for yer holiday, love?'

'What's the ice-cream budget?'

'If it means I get to North Marine Road then you can go

to town on the choc-ices.'

'Deal.'

Mrs Fuller was similarly ambushed when this cricket book was agreed, with the notion of a working holiday around the cricket, amplified by as many chips as were required and no expense spared over the B&B breakfast.

The reason that so many are drawn back to Scarborough is that it is a character in our lives and, over time, we have that familiar connection through those we meet and the touch points that bind us.

In the case of the Tindalls, they'd been trying for a baby and were on the IVF waiting list, but the prospect of an addition to the family became a fabulous reality, out of the blue.

News of the pregnancy broke the week before their maiden trip to the coast in 2007 and the couple went there for the visit of Somerset in the NatWest Pro40 League:

'I thought "Wow! Why did I never know about this place?" From that point, we associated Scarborough with good news.'

Their daughter, Molly, was born and the family returned to Scarborough the following year and every year since. This personal connection has even meant Helen has been converted from being mildly interested in cricket to being a Yorkshire County Cricket Club member. The Tindalls' short-stay pilgrimage includes a day for each of the three of them where they decide what to do. No guesses for where David opts for.

Conversely, there can be poignancy too and for the

Tindalls, David's dad passed away, with the Scarborough Cricket Festival being the last time the extended family were together. They were there for the Group B game of the Clydesdale Bank 40 in 2010 where Yorkshire snuck past Middlesex by five runs.

On a hot and sultry afternoon, a near-capacity crowd savoured a closely-fought 40 overs tussle book-ended by a Jacques Rudolph hundred and a miserly spell by Anthony McGrath. The Tindall clan did the usual things of walking the outfield in the break and going to stare meaningfully at the pitch.

Now, this is a must-do ritual and one I'm prone to indulge in myself. The thought process goes something like this. I think I'll go and stare at the wicket, cordoned off by rope, while it gets a good sweep and the lines get repainted. Others around me gawp meaningfully at the ground, looking for clues, assessing conditions and watching the ground staff like hawks. I then walk off, satisfied and yet absolutely none the wiser.

* * *

An email pinged into my inbox late one January morning from a Yorkshire fan who preferred anonymity given the deeply personal account that was laid bare over a thousand words. He spelled out a long association with the Scarborough Cricket Festival going back to the 1950s when his dad, a club cricketer for Saltburn, went every September.

For the purposes of this, let's call our raconteur Alan. In the first few years of going, Alan's dad met fans from Warwickshire and Leicestershire at the Festival who were to become lifelong friends, as well as his future wife, a keen cricket fan who hailed from Cudworth near Barnsley.

Alan's first Scarborough Cricket Festival was in 1965, when he was less than a year old. It was the year that the South Africans toured and Alan was placed in his carrycot behind the bar in the Carlsberg Lager tent so his parents could watch the cricket. The bar manager kept an eye on the baby although rumour has it that one of the South African Rowan brothers tried to ply him with lager at an early age.

'Over the years, I managed to bowl at Boycott on the outfield; saw my sister fall in love with Asif Iqbal of Kent when he gave her a piggyback off the field; was there for the first one-day international played at Scarborough; suffered a plague of greenfly one year; learnt how to hold a bat properly and watched countless games of cricket in the best ground in the world.'

In Alan's case, his parents met at the Festival in Scarborough so he wouldn't be here today were it not for the marvel of outground county cricket. His father passed away in 2018 and Alan was due to read the eulogy at the funeral when he emailed me to pass on his association with North Marine Road.

There was one paragraph that particularly hit home. Alan was in his dad's bedroom after he'd passed away and spotted a copy of *All Wickets Great and Small*, the cricket book I wrote about Yorkshire clubs, and the last Father's Day book Alan had given him.

It didn't look as if it had been finished, but well thumbed through and I hope it gave some enjoyment. Us writers plough on with the next article, column or book, rarely pausing to register what impact, if any, our work has on the world.

I happened to be going through a particularly rough spell of health that January and was questioning many things, not least my effect on the world and to what extent my cricket writing really makes any difference to people's lives. That email was a powerful reminder of how cricket connects and unites us and, somewhat selfishly, the last line about my book gave me a timely lift during a dark week.

* * *

Correspondence came in all shapes and sizes. One gentleman called Martin took the trouble to scan in pages from a document, written for his friends and family, that started with his debut visit to Scarborough Cricket Festival in 1964, aged nine, and tied that to a visit in 2015, a half-century later.

His family had moved from the industrial grime of Bradford and the reward was fresh air and endless sand, though being taken by his father to see the Australians at North Marine Road as a young boy did not make a fantastic first impression:

'We sat in the eastern terrace, surrounded by men in

suits and ties. The benches were long and uncomfortable and the men smoked incessantly, but I don't remember them drinking beer at all. Most had khaki canvas bags with them that held a thermos flask and sandwiches, tied in greaseproof paper.'

It was a well-crafted read and transported me back to a decade in Scarborough before I was born. Martin helped as a donkey boy on the beach, walking tourists up and down the sands with bridle in hand. Apparently, on the North Bay beach they were called Whiskey and Shamrock and on the South Bay, the donkeys were more of a cultural nod: John, Paul, George and Ringo.

Pleasingly, I was bombarded with emails and tales about the Festival, but Martin's was initially rather lost as he had only committed it to paper and then photographed it. My Apple Mac desktop kept wanting to flip his words on screen onto their side (computers always think they know best and can be bossy), which made reading more than a bit tricky.

Once deciphered, I was transported into another world. Martin recalls going to the Scarborough Cricket Festival and before he got his own junior membership, his group of school friends would duck in without paying and head for the members' and players' entrance at the rear of the pavilion.

'This was protected by an old man wearing a white coat and a bowler hat. His job was to loosen a rope that barriered the entrance when a player approached or a member showed his card. It was easy at these times to distract him and run behind his back!'

The membership cards were colour coded, so blue, yellow and red signified 1966 to 1968. They were collected from the Secretary's office up a steep staircase at the side of the pavilion, as Martin takes up the story:

'The Secretary was a Mr Midgely and he had stern, horn-rimmed glasses. You needed to be brave, I remember, to collect your card, but I valued mine so much that I kept them in a Christmas toffee tin, along with a Churchill crown and an extracted wisdom tooth, until my wife threw them out during a spring clean in 1980.'

* * *

Mick Pope is a cricket author, historian and previously long-standing Secretary for Wombwell Cricket Lovers Society, who have out-of-season talks at Ardsley Oaks Club in Barnsley. Back in the wet season of 1978, he had hoped to watch his first day of Test cricket at the age of 14, as Pakistan were at Headingley for the Third Test match.

His auntie Flo had arranged bus tickets to Leeds and when they arrived, rain had been falling for many hours. The Test and County Cricket Board (as it was back then) charged admission even if no play was possible and there were no refunds. Mick and Flo decided to risk it anyway and paid, but all they saw were empty stands and the umpires eventually called it off.

Scarborough was to come to the rescue soon after in a rain-reduced John Player League match. He ended up taking a ride in the back of the van belonging to his mate's dad, which had been cleared of the usual stock of jeans sold at various markets. Though the weather intervened again, North Marine Road delivered an adventure.

'Like now, Scarborough allowed youngsters and families onto the outfield and we were asked by South African Clive Rice to field a few balls for him. Wow, it hurt when the ball crashed into your hands, but I remember it still! We bagged a few autographs that day, Rice among them, and we also got to see Yorkshire win a 27-over per side game by six wickets.

'On the long journey home, we stopped at some pub for pop and crisps and arrived back very late that night. Scarborough was in my memory banks and the soggy Headingley trip a few weeks earlier was already forgotten!'

* * *

Videos (we're talking old-school VHS tapes) are another Aladdin's cave when it comes to bringing past Scarborough Cricket Festivals back to life. The enticing spools encased in bulky blocks of plastic now largely reside in outdated charity shops or stashed away in cupboards by Yorkshire cricket fans who recorded the White Rose on the telly many moons ago.

Jeremy Lonsdale, an author of early Yorkshire history books, told me how he'd chanced upon a video with two hours of footage from Yorkshire TV of a Yorkshire vs Leicestershire encounter in the 1989 Festival.

Yorkshire TV, the predecessor of ITV Yorkshire, had a yellow logo like a tick that had toppled over. Apparently, it's a fleur-de-lis chevron (whatever that is) though it speaks to my cultural references that my mind went to the top of a McDonald's 'M.'

The footage is something of a collector's item as it is from the lesser-known Ward Knockout Cup semi-final that Yorkshire won by three wickets. Jeremy was struck by the exuberance of David Bairstow when he was batting, talking and laughing to himself.

'The end of the Yorkshire innings sees DLB run out in rather silly fashion, stranded in the middle of the wicket not knowing which end to head for. Despite Yorkshire being close to winning and the match really of no significance, he looks absolutely furious with his partner. As he walks off, Arnie Sidebottom comes in and the two pretend to exchange blows with their bats. A nice little sequence.'

* * *

It was only when I dug deeper into the depths of my Gmail inbox folder that I found all kinds of correspondence that shed a light on individual moments of the Festival, performances or characters.

Brian Sanderson, a stalwart of the Yorkshire County Cricket Club Archives committee, sent me the menu from the 1930 Festival's Civic banquet and the official scorecard. The former commemorates the 50th Scarborough Cricket Festival and is held together with white ribbon.

There was a 13-course meal of which the latter five consisted entirely of booze from sherry to Croft's port. Presumably they needed all that alcohol to get through the numerous toasts from the King to the other royals then onto the Australian squad and the mayor. It's hard not to find the attempts at grandeur endearing. They ate 'Sole Frite a la Scarborough,' or fish and chips to us commoners.

I find adverts some of the best clues to what a decade was like. The designs and use of language, colour and font in the back pages of the menu is almost as revealing as any Tardis.

There was an advert for the retailer Boyes on Queen Street, with its 'fascinating show of fancy goods,' no less. A rather forlorn box underneath admits, 'This space is to let,' which is rather after the horse has bolted when it comes to advertising in the programme.

* * *

Back at the game, I met up with Scarborough's Secretary Colin Adamson, who retires after this Festival from the role he has filled since 1985 when Kent and Nottinghamshire were visitors to Scarborough in the Britannic Assurance County Championship. It would be his last hurrah and not a quiet one, judging by the fact that every time I saw him over the four days, he was hurrying off somewhere carrying a box.

In total, there have been ten Secretaries at Scarborough Cricket Club since Robert Baker's stewardship began in 1869. Colin's tenure spanned 1985 to 2018 and closed a chapter on the longest-serving official in that capacity.

As these things so often do, it began much earlier. Colin's association with Scarborough Cricket Club was initiated when his father Albert, who turned out for the club's 'A' team and Scarborough Reserves, would bring him to games: 'Saturday afternoons would be Dad taking me along while he played and then me playing with the sons and daughters. That was my first insight into cricket.'

When he was very young, the Adamson family didn't venture far for their holidays, choosing to attend each day of the Scarborough Cricket Festival rather than go further afield. Colin's first was in 1956 with Yorkshire vs Marylebone Cricket Club (MCC), the thrill of the T.N. Pearce's XI and the Gentlemen vs Players.

When he got a bit older, Colin would go to county matches on his own or with friends and sit on the Popular Bank, reinforcing his attachment to the place that would become his office for decades. After graduating from university, he'd wander down to the cricket club, even on non-match days as if magnetically drawn, and volunteer in the office.

Such persistence paid off and by February 1982, he was offered the job of Assistant Secretary, a role he had for about three years before taking over as Secretary from Lt Commander Henry (Harry) Wood in 1985.

What does the Secretary of Scarborough Cricket Club actually do? According to Colin, the short answer is anything and everything: 'The whole of the administration of the club together with the day-to-day bookkeeping and accountancy side of it.'

Being a club Secretary isn't for everyone at a small club, let alone a county outground with the history and heritage that comes with it. The appeal of the role was the inevitable focus around the Scarborough Cricket Festival, the visits of county teams and opportunities to have the cricket club and town in the spotlight.

Colin's enjoyment has always stemmed from the sense of familiarity, getting to know supporters who come year after year and welcoming them back as friends. That's not to say there haven't been worries and doubts:

'The financial side of the club has always been very real. Over the period of the 36 and a half years, we've had some very good outcomes from a financial point of view, but the demise of the cricket Festival, in the traditional sense, does have a significant impact.'

It's not something you say every day, but we turned our attention to insects. Believe it or not, bugs arriving in Scarborough in vast squadrons appears to be a not-too-infrequent occurrence. There are references to greenfly invasions at the cricket, but Colin is adamant that there was one year where it was ladybirds that caused the nuisance. The collective noun for them is a 'loveliness of ladybirds,' though, as Colin recalls, those attending the Festival were in for a shock.

'You would see them in these absolutely massive groups. It was very, very unusual. I've never come across it before or again. Quite bizarre. Particularly if you were wearing yellow, I seem to remember. You were the biggest attraction!'

* * *

Back to Monday's Festival cricket and it's after lunch, where Worcestershire are in total control and Daryl Mitchell has his third hundred of the season. The visitors are still only one wicket down and have now nudged into the lead at 235-1, with Moeen Ali looking equally serene.

With a degree of fortune, I am under cover, nosing at the cricket books for sale next to the bar when it starts to rain. It soon gets heavy enough to send the players and umpires scurrying off for an early tea. I find myself next to Ted, the bookseller from Leicestershire, who has been coming to Scarborough Cricket Club for the past decade.

Each year, he lays out his wares of second-hand, antiquarian and autographed books on wobbly trestle tables next to the beer barrels. He'll come for the first two days of a match and sell out much of his stock then head home, aware (as he told me) that his wife isn't that into cricket, though she does come along to lend a hand.

Ted's first Scarborough experience was in 1954 when he came to watch Yorkshire play the Canadians. He'd stay on North Marine Road where he could sit out and have his breakfast on the roof terrace. His bookselling business began as a hobby after starting to collect Wisdens and stumping up for a set that he then sold via *The Cricketer* magazine. His new business was born.

* * *

I found myself in the Bill Foord Enclosure when play began again. I stood with my back to the whitewashed wall to watch the first ball after tea as Yorkshire debutant Josh Poysden bowled to Moeen Ali from the Trafalgar Square End. Ali elegantly scooped it high and handsome in my direction.

I tried to track the ball's trajectory – because I sure as hell couldn't see the actual ball – and only spotted it as a very fast flash of red as it thudded into the wall right next to my head.

I reckon we're only talking a foot or so away, but I can't give you an exact distance as I had covered my head and performed a dainty skip. Two ladies seated at the end of a row pointed at me and covered their mouths with their hands, in shock, sympathy or, as is more likely, to hide a snort of laughter.

The evening session did not go Yorkshire's way as Moeen Ali reached his first century since April 2016 and Worcestershire reached 310-1 with a lead of 94. The gloom descended and, in the last half hour, I saw something I've not seen before: the Yorkshire faithful heading for the exit before the end.

Many had not returned after the rain break, but of those

who made it back, chairs were now packed up and flasks deposited in bags after a humbling day. It's rare indeed to only witness a single wicket fall in a day at Scarborough.

Chances had been few and far between and, to rub salt in the wounds, Matthew Fisher spilled a diving catch at the deep square leg boundary on the final ball of the day. It looked as if he caught it cleanly, but the ball popped out as his body hit the deck. If Yorkshire were seeking auspices, this summed it up.

Some fans had seen enough, or, as one man growled in the direction of the Yorkshire changing room while storming off towards the turnstiles:

'Ah'm not watchin' this roobish!'

As supporters disappeared out of the gates, I met up with Kevin Sharp, Worcestershire head coach, to ask him about his Yorkshire debut at Scarborough many moons ago. The left-handed batsman's career with Yorkshire spanned 1976 to 1991. He was capped in 1982 and received a benefit in 1991, finishing with 9,962 first-class runs from 218 matches for the White Rose.

He's in a good mood, as you'd expect him to be given the way the day has panned out. The Yorkshire County Cricket Club performance analyst Phil walks over with a laptop to explain why a couple of runs are going to be shaved off Worcestershire's total due to an error somewhere between the umpires signalling and the scorers. Kevin smiles and shrugs magnanimously.

Sharp's first-class debut was at Scarborough in 1976 against Northamptonshire who won by 198 runs, courtesy of a Geoff Cook hundred and seven second-innings wickets for Indian spinner Bishan Bedi.

'All my heroes were footballers. Cricketers weren't particularly, but it was quite clear, around 15 years old, that I was going to be a better cricketer than a footballer.'

Sharp was fast-tracked through the system playing for Yorkshire's age groups as a talented batsman and thinks he became the second-youngest player ever to play for the county behind Doug Padgett.

What was it like as a young cricketer entering that dressing room? 'Daunting. There were a lot of tough characters. Hard school, really. I was a cheeky little lad, but I soon got put in my place. In my first pre-season after the first week I knew where I stood. As a young player, it was sometimes better to listen than speak.

'I can remember thinking for my debut, "I hope I don't let anybody down." My parents were here to watch and I had a few nerves that I probably didn't have growing up.'

Players coming into any Yorkshire side have the bar set high, but particularly one still relatively near to the glory of the Sixties: 'In many respects, you had to be a team man, but you also had to be slightly single-minded. I think one of the hardest things playing for Yorkshire was the expectancy.'

Sharp played in an era where other counties had stolen a march on Yorkshire by embracing stellar overseas players, such as Viv Richards, Joel Garner, Barry Richards and Gordon Greenidge. It was a difficult period for Yorkshire with the club unable to replicate the success that had once felt commonplace.

Scarborough actually played its part in Sharp staying at Yorkshire for as long as he did, rather than moving to Worcestershire, whose Chairman, Duncan Fearnley, was keen on the player. It was at a time when Sharp had received his county cap, but was stuck in the Seconds and disillusioned.

The transfer never happened as Sharp returned to Yorkshire's first team and he cemented his place with 139 against Surrey at Scarborough in 1983; his highest County Championship innings, passing 4,500 first-class runs in the process.

I leave Kevin to more media interviews and head for the exit. It's funny how quickly a packed cricket ground can empty. There's now barely anyone here other than players dragging out their wheelie bags, journalists clutching recording devices and a few autograph-hunters lingering.

There is a sombre air to proceedings, from a Yorkshire perspective anyhow, but this is the reality of county cricket. You have good days and bad days, but you do the interviews, get up the next morning and go again. It jars, however, with the holiday vibe of Scarborough. Looking up at the Gods, it's a bleak, monochrome sky, as if the weather has decided enough's enough and is ushering us all out.

Our evening is the polar opposite, dining with friends at the Coffee Beans Cafe on Columbus Ravine, sharing laughs and stuffing ourselves to the gunnels. We happily lose a few hours and end up being the last ones out the door.

Tuesday morning:
Scores on the doors

After a breakfast of waffles bathing in a sea of maple syrup, Mrs Fuller and I took a stroll and wound our way down to the road that skirts along North Bay beach. Being before 9am, it was quiet with the occasional excited dog tearing along the sand. We stood there peacefully, took in hearty lungfuls of sea air and smiled. Sometimes, fresh air and a sea view is all that's really needed.

I took myself off to North Marine Road and up the stairs of the Pavilion's side entrance to meet Geoff, a man who has been coming to the Festival since 1945, a year he refers to as the Victory Festival.

Yorkshire faced a Royal Air Force XI at the end of August in a three-day match less than four months after the formal surrender of Germany in the Second World War. After the draw, Herbert Sutcliffe had played his last first-class match for Yorkshire to conclude on 50,670 runs, averaging 52.

Geoff is sat inside by the bar and has a navy blue blazer folded by his feet. It has a Scarborough Cricket Club patch sewed on the breast; the motif with crossed cricket bats was sourced in the 1980s from the outfitter Greensmith and Thackwray in town. He sports a navy tie with bands in the club's shade of orange.

I didn't enquire as to his age, it matters not, though there can't be many who have been coming to Scarborough Cricket Club longer than Geoff. A captivating man to listen to; leaning in towards me, with piercing eyes and shock white hair, he would offer up stories and then in the same breath, say: 'Well, I don't know if any of this is of interest.'

His memory is crisp and his commitment to Scarborough Cricket Club unwavering, serving twice on the committee, selling limited edition stamps, Festival programmes and scorecards on the front gate. Geoff has even been given permission to bury his ashes on the ground: 'So I can haunt them,' he says, turning to fix me with a penetrating stare before laughing.

* * *

I hunker down in the press box for the morning, scribbling notes in a hand that has got progressively lazier over time. Fresh from university, it was a tidy, rounded style, easily legible and precise. As time spent online has mushroomed, so our need to actually pick up a pen and write has become redundant. I haven't forgotten how to write entirely, you'll be pleased to know, but it is now a scrawl and I find myself starting to write a word, but the second half becomes a squiggle.

As I decipher my own hieroglyphics, I glance up to

survey the room. Yorkshire scorer John Potter is signalling that he has seen the umpire's signal by flicking a switch and sparking a lightbulb into life. He's wearing a red Emirates cap and, at first glance, I think it's a US Republican 'Make America Great Again' cap which makes me do a double-take.

John began scoring county games in the crowd at Scarborough and would go round to check his figures with Ted Lester, Yorkshire's scorer for 21 years. An opportunity subsequently fell into Potter's lap: 'Out of the blue, Ted rang me and said, "Would you like to do the away scoring?" It was basically who you knew rather than what you knew!'

John's scoring duty for the Yorkshire first team began in 1988, initially doing the away matches until he took over full-time in 1993. He told me that 2018 was his 31st season and there's no-one left on the county circuit that John started with. That all adds up to a shed-load of games, in the region of 1,100 to 1,200 by his estimation. Give or take, that's the equivalent of scoring eight hours a day, every day, for a full year.

Back in 1993, it was the heady days of early computerised scoring, described by John as hit and miss, but when he first started the county scores were still phoned through and an up-to-date scorecard would be read out. He fondly remembers the social side too with lavish lunches laid on as he'd share a bottle of wine with umpires John Hampshire and Barrie Leadbeater, firm favourites at the Festival.

One of Potter's highlights was the Northern Electric Trophy between Yorkshire and Durham that ran between 1993 and 1999. There were Northern bragging rights at stake: 'Myself and Brian Hunt from Durham used to joke that whoever won it would go through Scarborough on an open top bus!'

He recalls how the press box at Scarborough used to have windows that you could open to be cooled on a hot day and also listen to the sounds outside: 'One year, a pigeon flew in and I eventually picked it up and threw it out which led to the headline: Potter gets his hands on a bird.'

Our conversation, which actually took place as John was setting up for the Roses T20 match at Headingley, turns to a story about Buckingham Palace. I'm curious if scorers get the same recognition as players do after major trophies are secured. In one sense, the scorer hasn't worked any differently to normal and yet it's common in other sports that match officials see some kind of nod to the occasion.

Under John's watchful eye, Yorkshire County Cricket Club have picked up three County Championships and he was presented with a medal by Rachael Heyhoe-Flint in 2001.

The Yorkshire party first met HRH The Duke of Edinburgh who, as patron of the Lord's Taverners, has held a ceremony at Buckingham Palace for the county champions since 1973. The following year, Potter received a scorer's medal as part of Yorkshire's Cheltenham & Gloucester Trophy win over Somerset in 2002 and he was also given a winner's medal by the then-coach Wayne Clark.

To listen to a county scorer in action is to appreciate they are meticulous, numerical wizards; guardians of the nuts and bolts of cricket. The little things and yet the things that matter the most. A bit like a wicketkeeper who has to watch every single ball of an innings, a scorer can't drift off for half an hour and start salivating over whether it will be the rhubarb crumble or ginger pudding at tea.

They are not only indispensable for the ongoing mechanics of a cricket match, but in the press box, John will throw out timely statistical goodies, seized upon by the journalists: Ballance's fifty came off nine deliveries and broke six tiles in the pavilion roof; No-one has scored more leg-glances while wearing spikes the colour of satsumas; That lad has exceeded the number of forward defences in a calendar year, set by Lord Hawke in 1888. You get the picture.

* * *

I awake from my reverie and Worcestershire progress to 405 before losing their second wicket as Mitchell is out for 178. I'm stood by the edge of the pavilion and the Yorkshire fans across the whole ground give generous and prolonged applause.

With a possible England recall the obvious theme, Moeen Ali might capture the headlines, but Mitchell's seven-hour stay has been the foundation stone and the

Yorkshire faithful appreciate a batsman who drops anchor and refuses to budge.

The tally of 405 rings bells and it comes to me. Graeme Hick once scored that all on his own for Worcestershire at Taunton back in 1988. Living close to Somerset's home ground at the time meant that there was a feast of county cricket on the doorstep – though I wasn't there for Hick's landmark.

As it stands, the only equation to figure out for the visitors now is: when to declare? Consensus in the press box is that a lead of 250 will be a mountain for Yorkshire, but Worcestershire's declaration doesn't come.

Lunch arrives with Worcestershire in the enviable position of 479-3 and I make my way around to the marquee where I've been invited to attend the Scarborough Borough Council's Civic Lunch. It is pleasant and a completely different world to the one I normally inhabit.

As I tuck into a selection of puddings, surprisingly abstemious for me given others wobble past with heaving platefuls, Worcestershire are gorging themselves out in the middle. Yorkshire are huffing and puffing their way through, workmanlike, but waiting like the rest of us for the signal from the visitors' changing room to call it quits.

While the nuts and bolts of the drama out in the middle revolves around wickets, runs, strike rates and averages, there is a fringe Festival, if you like, taking place too. My thoughts turn to the world of business where cricket at Scarborough provides a backdrop to deals being done.

Business as usual

I was invited to the marquee lunch by Jim Dillon who has been Chief Executive of Scarborough Borough Council since 2006.

The Scarborough Cricket Festival is not just about clinching County Championships, but landing commercial deals too, and what better man to offer a snapshot of how important the Festival is to the town?

'Being Scottish, I never knew anything about cricket before I came to Scarborough. I used to get mixed up between cricket and fox hunting. I knew it was something English people did!'

His first experience at the Festival was over a decade ago with a move to the town from being the Ipswich Borough Council corporate director, and he gradually began to develop a genuine interest in the game. It turns out that conversations over cricket can act as the glue for regional prosperity.

'It's a phenomenal event for us. Not only does it attract visitors into the town, it acts as the biggest networking event I've ever come across, anywhere.' Over a few days, the movers and shakers from across Yorkshire and those passionate about Scarborough are all there at North Marine

Road.

Jim reckons: 'I've managed to foster more deals through Scarborough Cricket Festival than anything else. We've probably had about half a billion pounds investment in Scarborough in the last ten years – and a lot of that is down to the Festival.'

Scarborough Borough Council take tables in the marquee at the Festival and invite investors who have expressed an interest in the borough. There is something about business conducted away from the office that can help make things happen. A Friday afternoon meeting at the town hall might run the risk of being cancelled, whereas a day at the cricket is sacrosanct. It's about connections, introductions and building relationships. Everyone is there, whether finishing a beer in the tent or relaxing on a striped deckchair outside.

'The one thing about Scarborough is there is a Scarborough PLC and we all work together, whether it's the council, the business community or communities such as the rugby club and cricket club. The Festival is a communications tool within the town where all the people who are trying to do things and work together throughout the year come together. It's like a Congress or Assembly,' he reckoned.

Jim fostered a friendship with butcher Tony Gibson through the Festival and can recall the annual pork pie contest at the Leeds Arms pub, a popular haunt for cricket fans after a day's play. At some point, Jim became one of the 20 or so entrants who display their finest pies for judging in December, with some middling results and even a surprise third place after throwing it all together at the last minute one year.

Typically, he'd make the pie on the Thursday ahead of weekend judging to give the gelatine time to set, but one year, Jim phoned Tony Gibson in a state of panic on the Thursday evening having had no time to conjure up his finest baking efforts.

Tony saved the day and turned up with what was essentially a bumper pork pie kit with prime meat:

'All I had to do was stick it together, and of course my conscience was bothering me, but I put it in and I came 19th! I had sleepless nights before thinking I was going to be caught out, as Tony had told me that this pork pie was too good to even sell in the shop, it would only be for special guests!'

There is a cautionary tale in there somewhere about producing your own pies (I've bowled a few down the years) though Tony's award-winning credentials, both as butcher as well as player, coach and chairman at Scarborough Cricket Club are surely beyond reproach.

* * *

From pies to best buys, I thought I'd briefly explore a name synonymous with Scarborough Cricket Festival and share an insight into its past, present and future.

Department chain Boyes started as a Scarborough business in 1881 and their association with the

Scarborough Cricket Festival goes back to the 1890s when they would put an advert on the scorecards; something they've continued to do ever since.

It was in the form of a pictorial postcard and there's one proudly displayed at Boyes' Havers Hill head office in Scarborough of the 1903 Australian team, along with a picture of Yorkshire's batting duo Tunnicliffe and Brown in front of a scoreboard reading 378-1.

If you're not familiar with the eccentricities of shopping at Boyes then you're in for a treat. In the age of Amazon, when you can get just about anything delivered to your door in the blink of an eye, you might think a department store risks going the way of Woolworths.

But, here's the thing. Much as the Scarborough Cricket Festival has its appeal for not changing much, so too does one of its principal sponsors. There are products at Boyes that even Amazon doesn't sell. A trip to one of its cavernous, multi-floor bazaars is to lose yourself, literally and figuratively, in everything from reading glasses to Victoria Mint Imperials.

If you're in desperate need of anti-bacterial poo bags (for dogs, just to clarify) at the same time as wanting a pot of Dulux emulsion, then Bob's your uncle. It's easy to be glib, but seriously, I love the place. Their choice of 30,000 products is somewhat overwhelming, but then it's probably only me who takes a map and compass to happily spend a day inside.

My virgin experience of Boyes was in Bradford and it confirmed that there's still a place in my heart for a shop where you need to ask for a key to the toilet. The cafe is situated behind the lingerie section so you have to fight your way through lace bras to be rewarded with a cup of tea.

As far as I could tell, its hours of business were delightfully specific: we are open for 40 minutes from 10.15am on a Wednesday and then you may dine after 3.51pm on Friday afternoon. You are greeted by a lectern, further suggesting this is not your usual cafe experience. The ladies who run it are a hoot and it's one of my favourite places to dunk bread into a bowl of soup in the city.

Tim Boyes is a Director in the family business and has been a keen supporter of county cricket at Scarborough over the years.

'As a schoolboy, I used to come down from Teeside on the train when you could do the full trip direct to Scarborough. A fond memory is of the tourist team putting their blazers on at lunchtime to walk across to the marquee. They were very giving of their time. I remember meeting (West Indies cricketers) Sobers and Worrell, schoolboy heroes in those days.'

He was invited to be President of Scarborough Cricket Club, a spell that included the 2004 Festival, stayed on the committee for years after and is also a trustee of the club for good measure. Boyes always had an end-of-summer company sale in early September and Tim would get letters from wives of cricket fans asking when it was happening so couples could co-ordinate cricket-watching with sale-shopping.

In case you're wondering, Boyes caters for family T20 on the beach rather than the serious connoisseur who examines cricket bats for straightness of grains and grade of willow. Selling plastic bats and baseball caps, W. Boyes and Co. Ltd is bucking the trend of some retailers who are fighting a constricting high street, with Tim due to open new stores in Retford and Worksop as we spoke.

* * *

While lasting relationships with sponsors like Boyes is part of what keeps Scarborough Cricket Club ticking, it recognises the commercial strides needed to create a 52-week business rather than relying purely on the Yorkshire matches.

The Rubik's Cube to solve is transforming a county cricket venue that relies so heavily on the income from the Scarborough Cricket Festival into a place that attracts visitors and earns all year round – even when it's dark by 4pm and cricket couldn't be further from the mind.

To that end, there's been everything from murder mystery evenings to a Bavarian traditional Oompah band. The traditional Festival dinner in the marquee is also a popular mainstay while the cricket is in town.

Nudging the local community that North Marine Road is always open as a venue is a drip-drip process. Speaking to the club's Chief Executive Rob Richtering, there's a dose of realism when I ask him what Scarborough Cricket Club would look like without county cricket to sustain it:

'Luxury flats and the ground somewhere else!'

I meet up with Chairman Paul Harrand and talk about the financial realities the club face.

'We control the controllables. You can't do anything about the players once they cross the boundary line. Last year (2017) was a pretty bad year for us. The Essex game finished in two days and we took a hit on that. The balance sheet showed a £70,000 loss purely based on ten days' cricket becoming five days' cricket. You're trying to run a 365-day business on five days of cricket. It's not a great business plan!'

Aside from the match finishing before the end of the scheduled four days, the other perennial worry concerns whole days lost to rain. The club must assume that cricket will happen and staff the ground accordingly, which can be an expensive damp squib.

Yorkshire County Cricket Club earn, regardless of climate, for taking their team to North Yorkshire, so Scarborough Cricket Club can usually be found crossing every digit that it will be dry. The hosts rely on bumper attendances and overflowing beer to top up the coffers.

The soggy summer of 2012 was a case in point and represented something of an annus horribilis for Scarborough. From the fans' perspective, Yorkshire claimed 19 Championship points with a two-wicket victory over Gloucestershire – but two days were lost to rain. Chairman-at-the-time Bill Mustoe reckoned that equated to a £20,000 loss per day.

* * *

For a club that has a hard-won reputation for maintaining the status quo, Scarborough doesn't half have lots of potential change to contend with.

Paul stresses the close bond between Yorkshire County Cricket Club and Scarborough Cricket Club. In Yorkshire's Chief Executive Mark Arthur, he seems to have an ally who knows that the Yorkshire membership hold Scarborough dear.

Harrand will be in charge of negotiations with Yorkshire as the sand runs down on a ten-year agreement that goes through until 2020. There is no question of county cricket stopping at Scarborough, given the crowds it attracts, but the air of uncertainty swirling on many fronts does nothing for peace of mind on the coast.

How much county cricket Scarborough gets is a worry and the shifting tectonic plates of the domestic schedule are pause for thought and concern. The new 100-ball competition called The Hundred, for which Headingley is one of the venues, could provide both opportunity and a knock-on effect for later Scarborough Cricket Festivals.

At the time of writing, no-one knows when this will be inked in for and what the ramifications will be on an already hectic schedule. With only a year to go, that makes long-term planning by counties and associated grounds impossible.

As I see it, venues like Scarborough Cricket Club have no particular power to do more than grumble over their allocation, but the continuation of staging two four-day games with Yorkshire by the sea is clear-cut and to everyone's benefit.

Where it could be more negative is if The Hundred ends up being in August so the Festival might need to be moved. You can imagine the reaction by those who have been coming to Scarborough since the dawn of time. As far as I can tell, it's nearly always been scheduled during the summer holidays and Scarbados in May has less appeal.

The timing of the Festival might seem unnecessarily pedantic, but it's something we both chew on. Paul confided that the rumour doing the rounds was that the County Championship may not be scheduled at all in August in future to make way for the ECB's new competition. I might have let slip a comment that, at this rate, the supposed showpiece for county cricket might take place in March and October before long.

The Scarborough Cricket Festival has been played in other months (it was moved to July in 1997 to try to yield better gate receipts) so it would not be complete anarchy, but if it comes to pass, it will go down like an under-done Yorkshire pudding.

What will irk fans of four-day cricket is that it further lends weight to the notion that the County Championship can be sliced, diced and shunted anywhere to make way for any other competition.

Moving it back to July will not cause too much consternation as the school holidays will have broken up, but if the new T16.6666667 is in August, the T20 Blast would have to be in July and, well, it can make your head spin trying to figure it out.

On *Cricket Yorkshire*, I've talked before to Professor Mike Wright at Lancaster University Management School who, with the aid of a computer programme, has been the man behind crunching the ECB's fixture conundrum and attempting to make all the permutations work as best they can.

The Lancaster University website lists Mike's research interests as: 'the development and analysis of metaheuristic methods and their implementation to practical problems including sports timetabling and employee scheduling.'

That appetite for crunching the numbers may be sorely tested with the dimension of a fourth cricket tournament involving counties, but I wonder what happens when all the preferences and requests are inputted, if the answer is 'computer says no!'

As Paul Harrand put it during our conversation: 'It's not inconceivable that the Festival could move to June. It would be a seismic shift because the Yorkshire cricketing public are creatures of habit. They probably book ten years in advance at the boarding houses!'

By the time you read this, it might all be much clearer, but while fans remain in the dark, Scarborough Cricket Club don't get to plan too far ahead either.

They are taking the view of ruling nothing out and nothing in, reacting to whatever is presented to them. Admirable though that is, it doesn't lend itself to a long-term strategic vision if you're waiting for the ECB to decide if the few days of cricket that dictate the survival of your club will be in April or August.

Naturally, with the ICC Cricket World Cup in 2019 on its way, Harrand had his fingers crossed that Scarborough could be the immediate beneficiary as Yorkshire stage part of the global cricket roadshow in Leeds. But as you may know by now, getting additional county games in 2019 was not to be.

Instead, York Cricket Club was given the honour of hosting its debut first-class game at Clifton Park, in part because of the high concentration of Yorkshire members in the York area and the excellent reports of the wicket and facilities. Another outground for Yorkshire is to be applauded, but it adds to the competition for Scarborough. What North Marine Road has over York and other outgrounds is the existing credit in the bank with supporters:

'We're very lucky to have the support of the cricketing public and we never under-estimate that. I think it's quite humbling that people do turn up in their thousands to come and watch county cricket.'

* * *

One thread of our conversation that will hearten many is the enthusiasm for expanding the Scarborough Cricket Festival beyond its current four days. Paul references the Cheltenham Cricket Festival as a model to learn from, albeit not directly comparable as Gloucestershire County

Cricket Club organise it from their Bristol headquarters.

The 2018 Cheltenham Cricket Festival ran for two weeks in July at Cheltenham College during which there were two County Championship matches, two T20 Blast games and a Women's Super League fixture. Paul's face lights up as he outlines the beauty of a lengthened block of cricket activity with the ability to then put together a programme of off-the-field events too.

At Cheltenham College, there was a members' cricket forum, cricket memorabilia market, barbecue and quiz night, as well as a host of guests for question and answer sessions. There is definitely appetite at Scarborough to replicate this and actually wind back the clock a little to when the Festival was longer and had a lot more going on.

For Paul, who played at Scarborough in the Nineties, captained the Seconds and had some first-team outings too, it matters what happens next. He was promoted from Vice Chairman when Bill Mustoe stepped down and asked him to take the tiller. Harrand admits he thought long and hard about it, but there is scope to usher in the next chapter.

'My philosophy, from league chairman to what I'm doing now, is to try and make a difference. If you can and leave things in a better state than you found them; if you can do that, you haven't done a bad job. This is, by far, the biggest challenge I've ever had. Bill, my predecessor, will always say that Scarborough gets into your blood and it does.'

Paul remembers how the regionalisation of the vast network of Yorkshire club cricket was no piece of cake. It involved restructuring and ensuring four ECB Premier Leagues, with feeder leagues, gave a clear pathway, aiming to improve the quality of recreational cricket over time. That involved hundreds of meetings, but the Scarborough project is another level of administration again.

The cold reality of keeping everything afloat, analysing profit and loss, allied with the blend of paid staff and volunteers, makes for sleepless nights. There can't be enough hours in the day.

* * *

We turn our attention to the thorny topic of membership and the fact that Scarborough Cricket Club's is well down.

There's a loyalty to cricket at Scarborough but that only stretches so far and a reduced amount of cricket, allied with some poor results that further shave play down, means fans often opt to pay on the gate with the flexibility of assessing the position of the match and the weather.

Scarborough Cricket Club plan to address that by offering more attractive packages with incentives, discounts and extras to try to arrest the slump. As a trend, Scarborough's membership has been falling since the 1960s, with it noted as 4,527 in 1961, but down to 3,109 by 1970 and 2,135 by 1985. It stands today around the thousand-mark for 2018.

Of course, you choose to subscribe to a club or a service either as a sort of patronage with little expected in return or, in this case, take advantage of Scarborough Cricket

Club's membership benefits and the prospect of county cricket by the sea.

It becomes a question of simple maths and value. Is paying up front better than handing over money at the turnstiles? That will depend on the amount of county cricket awarded to Scarborough. Eight days currently equates to £80, as it's a tenner per day on the turnstiles, so a membership costing £95 might struggle to stand up to scrutiny.

However, a full member has the perk of access to all parts of the ground for all matches and the club is looking at building in bonuses for the 2019 Festival and beyond, such as money off the Festival dinner, offers with local businesses and discounted prices in the Pavilion Bar.

Does it matter that Scarborough Cricket Club's membership is falling? It remains an important factor in their finances and there's a distinction between those who are Scarborough members and Yorkshire County Cricket Club members; the latter have access to all Yorkshire CCC matches at North Marine Road.

We wrap things up discussing how the cricket ground may change in future, investment notwithstanding; a hospitality and office complex as part of a new stand (where the West Stand currently is) remains on the radar. Alternatively, a phase one option is a stand with a bar and groundsman's office. No world exclusives were revealed, unfortunately.

One school of thought is that the area where the marquee currently stands could be tarmacked with a new entrance that would be accessible for the Sky TV trucks. Now, that would be game-changing. You'd lose the marquee and the deckchairs outside, but gain global exposure and the ability to charge more to sponsors and advertisers as a result.

The ambition is there, but it all boils down to finding the funds to make some of these ideas actually become reality, allied with how many days of cricket Yorkshire allocate to Scarborough. If I sound like a stuck record, the health and wealth of the Festival can be seen in those very stark terms.

Though the club isn't holding any debt and they own the ground, the optimistic mood is tinged with caution, if I can put it like that. Who can blame them? Scarborough without county cricket is inconceivable, but there are enough variables, from the weather to which games they are allocated in future, to keep everyone on their toes.

Tuesday afternoon: Declaration and survival mode

Moeen Ali reaches the second double hundred of his career and the intention is pretty clear: to crush Yorkshire's energy and belief before unleashing the bowlers. With the full quota of overs unlikely and bad light a threat, Worcestershire appear to be a little greedy, but time will tell if the strategy pays off.

Ali eventually falls for 219, the highest innings by any visiting batsman in Championship cricket at North Marine Road and Worcestershire finally declare on 572-7. That's a lead of 356, which is more than Yorkshire have managed in any first-class innings in 2018. Yorkshire's bowlers can reflect on what might have been, particularly in the first hour of Worcestershire's innings where the White Rose didn't get the rub of the green, but they now face a scrap for survival.

The bowling figures never tell the full picture, but they reflect how the spin of Poysden and Lyth shared 44.2 overs and went at over five an over.

* * *

I take myself off to the Boundary Hotel on North Marine Road with its distinctive balcony that juts out over the cricket ground and offers guests a prime spot in which to catch some rays and some overs. I sink into the sofa and chat to owners Steve and Kate who only bought the business in April, swapping the stress of a Prison Service career with looking after customers and their particular needs.

As we talk, their spaniel Jack (at a guess, I'm rubbish with dog breeds) sits on the floor in front of me nuzzling a tennis ball and looking at me with big eyes that silently pine for play and attention. Apparently, the cricket fans that have stayed for the Surrey and Worcestershire games have been low maintenance, but like things a certain way.

They show me the bar area with its painting of W.G. Grace and a statue of a left-handed batsman donated by a guest, which has since been nicknamed 'Hedley' (after Hedley Verity, the slow left-arm bowler for Yorkshire and England).

The topic of the pressure of cooked breakfasts comes up. I sure wouldn't want to do it. It's the challenge of getting everything out on time and hot without the bacon looking like it's lost a battle with a flamethrower and the eggs still clucking and walking around the plate.

At the mention of eggs, Steve rolls his eyes and tells how his absolute nightmare was getting to grips with poached eggs. We've all been there. Get it wrong and you serve something akin to a watery eyeball. As luck would have it, their very first guest asked for poached eggs, but the B&B Gods were smiling, it turned out ok and the new management of the Boundary Hotel were up and running.

After a brief trip onto the balcony, where a collection of fans avidly study the cricket and glance up in my direction, as if daring me to interrupt this sacred space, it's time to wish Steve, Kate and Jack adieu.

* * *

Yorkshire face a mammoth task to save this game and not add Worcestershire to the list of Surrey, Somerset, Essex and Middlesex who have beaten them here in recent years. Batting time is something Yorkshire have struggled with, but they need to drop anchor and, if needs be, bore the hell out of the opposition and those who've stayed to see how their team responds.

Psychologically, how a batsman approaches this kind of batting is something I find fascinating. I've done enough interviews with professional cricketers to know that the answer would typically be: each ball and no further. Defend, frustrate, repeat.

Breaking down time into manageable chunks and ticking it off is the skill of any cricketer looking to bat a long time. So says the number eleven whose only fifty in any form of cricket in a career spanning 30 years was at an inter-club friendly that no-one remembers.

Yorkshire's need is for dogged attrition, but I can still picture a game in the Dales Council Cricket League where my team were put to the sword to the tune of 400 runs in 40 overs. It was oppressively hot. The ball was hit so often into the Leeds & Liverpool Canal (and every adjoining postcode) that it appeared to have been chewed within an inch of its life by a dog boasting overactive gums.

When it came to our turn to bat, I think we drew straws. That can be the only explanation for my elevation up the batting order. Some of the bowlers went off to sit in a dark room never to emerge. We were utterly frazzled and in urgent need of aftersun and a long, cool drink.

Instead, we had to summon up the fight to face a battery of hyped fast bowlers who'd just broken a tonne of individual, club and league batting records. I'd like to say that we stoically batted out our overs and narrowly lost by a few runs. I can't find the scorecard online, so let's just go with that, shall we?

The point to this irreverent amble down memory lane is that Yorkshire are in survival mode. Their only goal must be to see out the rest of the day without losing any wickets or with minimal damage to their top six. Which is all well and good except a County Championship encounter is a test of physical endurance as well as mental toughness; both of which might reasonably be frayed after 139.2 overs in the field.

Worcestershire fail to break through with the pace of Parnell and Tongue, but Moeen Ali enters the fray after 13 overs and traps Adam Lyth lbw. The scoreboard reads 37-

1. It becomes worse for the home side as the Worcestershire captain bags a second wicket soon after as Harry Brook departs for 16.

After tea, Yorkshire continue to lose wickets and Kane Williamson can only watch from the other end as Moeen Ali's phenomenal match continues to delight the away fans. Gary Ballance is caught in the slip cordon for 19 and Tom Kohler-Cadmore is out lbw. 116-4. Not good.

The notion of stamina is forefront in my mind, not least because Moeen Ali has batted for 380 minutes and shows little inclination for surrendering the ball. It is a dreadful position for Yorkshire, but as long as the world-class pedigree of Kane Williamson is out there, you just never know.

There's an absorbing passage of play that pits Williamson, 10,000 first-class runs and a Test average of 50, against the speed of Dillon Pennington, not yet 21 and with a mere handful of four-day games to his name. The Worcestershire fast bowler is striving for his fifth wicket of the match and though he doesn't yet manage it in this spell, it's noticeable how he beats the bat of one of the world's finest international cricketers.

At around 4.30pm, Moeen Ali is bowling to Kane Williamson from the Pavilion End when the New Zealander suddenly steps away from the crease. Moeen pauses in his run-up. A gentleman in a cream jacket and trousers is ambling across from the West Stand. Rather than skirt around the circumference, he's opted to save time and slice off the corner, so play has to be halted.

He's either oblivious to the fact that being on the pitch has forced an interruption or simply doesn't mind. Either way, there's a surreal minute that passes as everyone in the ground watches this man make his slow but merry way onwards.

Eventually, he crosses the boundary rope and waves at the crowd in the North Stand who are none too pleased. I may be doing him a great disservice, but the spectator had come from the direction of the hospitality marquee and there was more than a passing chance that he was well sauced.

It was to be a brief, light-hearted moment before the clouds rolled in for Yorkshire as Kane Williamson had a flash at a wide delivery from Wayne Parnell and trudged off for 61, shaking his head. A thoroughly galling day for Yorkshire fans concluded with Tim Bresnan's six-ball duck, as Worcestershire were able to reflect on a day that had gone perfectly.

Worcestershire (572-7 declared) needed to claim Yorkshire's last four wickets on the final day to wrap up a handsome victory. The home side (216 & 140-6) had to score 216 runs just to make the opposition bat again. It left those of a White Rose persuasion pinning their hopes either on a meteorological gift in the shape of a North Sea storm, or a rearguard of epic proportions from David Willey and the Yorkshire tail.

Wednesday:
Lowering the Yorkshire flag

Wednesday begins with a walk up Queen's Parade, past the white Victorian facade of the Clifton Hotel, where war poet Wilfred Owen stayed from 1917. Occupying a turret room, he wrote his first poem 'Miners' while looking out onto the frothing North Sea.

Mrs Fuller is accompanying me, it's a sunny morning and we take a moment to sit on a dark green bench, marvelling at the acrobatics of the seagulls. According to the RSPB, herring gulls are the permanent residents of Scarborough and many other coastal towns. Noisy, boisterous and alarmingly large, with pink legs and a red spot on their beak, I now know who was responsible for an audacious aerial attack on my chips on a recent trip to Whitby.

Our bench has a plaque that reads: 'Rest awhile remembering Albert and Madge who loved Scarborough so much.' It's a lovely way to honour someone's life and untold numbers will have relaxed there, watching the sea and taking in the curve of the beach round to the remains of the castle.

We take the winding path down, across the road and onto the beach itself. There's something holistic and immensely satisfying to stand just back from the lapping shoreline and gaze out to sea. The sun glints off the waves and there is nothing between here and Denmark. I reckon we're roughly in line with the Danish town of Klitmoller.

Google thought I could walk the 805 miles via Hull and Rotterdam, but there is an alternative. Apparently, it can take about 30 hours to cover the 580 kilometres from Scarborough to Esbjerg in a Viking longboat (if you have one) and then a three-hour drive up to Klitmoller. Well, now you know.

* * *

Suitably refreshed, I get to Scarborough Cricket Club with more than an hour before play. It is free admission, but the crowd will be thin, with the expectation that this could all be wrapped up by lunch. I wander aimlessly (as is my way at many a cricket ground) and find myself in the steep, upper reaches of the North Stand.

A couple are doing a word puzzle together and checking how many they've each managed to find from the grid. Their son plays for Glasshoughton Cricket Club firsts in the Pontefract League and they've been coming to the cricket at Scarborough for years.

As play starts, I meet a photographer friend John Heald over in the tea room. He starts with a story of being struck by a ball from the bat of the prolific West Indian all-rounder

Garfield Sobers as a child.

It happened before the start of a Test match between England and the West Indies at Headingley. Garry Sobers walked to young master Heald and checked he was ok before enquiring if he had an autograph book, which John did.

The West Indian, whose world-record score of 365 was achieved at the age of 21 and famously deposited Malcolm Nash for six sixes in an over, disappeared into the changing room. Sobers returned with an autograph book packed with all of the players.

John also smiles at the memory of a Scarborough Cricket Festival where the Pakistani bowler Sarfraz Nawaz kept dropping catches. After another one had gone to ground, Derek Randall ran off, picked up a large wire mesh rubbish bin, brought it onto the field and handed it to Nawaz. John captured that moment on camera, with spectators and fielders laughing and the umpire looking on bemused.

His photos are a reminder not just of the cricket, but of past eras and how things used to be, from buildings to fashion. Nawaz actually fielded for a delivery stood inside that bin in a joke that reflected the light-hearted camaraderie with which some Festival games were contested at the time.

There's a priceless image of Worcestershire's head coach Kevin Sharp being given his man-of-the-match award in 1983 by Scarborough's President Brian Johnston. Sharp had hit 139 in the drawn game against Surrey, passing his highest first-class score at the time of 125. He's posing for the camera with a mighty perm.

John also had a Geoffrey Boycott tale up his sleeve. He wasn't the first to tell me that the Yorkshire batsman would get kids to bowl at him before the start of a match at Scarborough. He'd put a coin on the stumps with the instruction that, 'If you get me out, you can keep it.' Of course, no one ever did.

Such is the ease with which the conversations develop that we almost forget about the cricket. When the wickets start to fall, which doesn't take long, it all goes pear-shaped for Yorkshire. David Willey, who is captaining Yorkshire's County Championship side for the first time, will not look back on his leadership debut with much fondness and was bowled by Moeen to precipitate the final slump to defeat.

Matthew Fisher fell in the same over and at 149-8, I hurriedly promised to catch up with John over winter. I made my way around to sit square of the wicket on the first row of the Popular Bank. Yorkshire's demise lasted all of ten overs as Dillon Pennington nipped out Brooks then Poysden and Worcestershire won by an innings and 186 runs.

* * *

There had been something inevitable about the last rites of play. I walked over to sit by the pavilion and quietly observe what the reaction might be. A red-faced fan with a white bucket hat stomped past and shouted 'ROOBISH!'

at the Yorkshire dressing room. Feeling it required no further elaboration, he carried on his not-so-merry way as others looked a little embarrassed.

There was no angry clutch of Yorkshire supporters congregating to stage a protest, but then the direction – if not the final result – had been set ever since Worcestershire had struck their highest first-class score against Yorkshire, comfortably eclipsing a record that had stood for over a hundred years.

The home dressing room stays closed. Occasionally, a member of the support staff comes out, but the scene behind that white door remains off limits. Minutes tick by and it's tempting to ponder what's being said by Andrew Gale or senior players to chastise, motivate or draw a line under the performance.

In front of this private meeting, members are packing up their things, many having called their plastic seat home for the past three-and-a-bit days. Bags are filled with empty sandwich boxes, newspapers creased into compliance at the cricket pages, coats and hats located during a final sweep of surroundings.

Two girls with ponytails wearing black Worcestershire Rapids T20 shirts wait patiently on the outfield for signatures and perk up as Worcestershire's players begin to emerge. A pint-sized young fan, in a black Yorkshire Vikings top and long green shorts, hovers at the side gate to the pavilion with his mum. It is, she tells me, a routine they're well used to after games here.

'So, which players are you after then?'

No hesitation.

'Ballance. Willey. Williamson.'

A pause to think in an otherwise breathless shopping list of must-get signatures.

'Ok, if you could only get one player, who would it be?'

The answer is quickly delivered and unexpected, given it's none of the current or past internationals on show, but one of Yorkshire's younger squad members.

'Tatts!' is the reply as his eyes light up, after having begun the conversation shyly, half hidden in his mother's coat.

The Yorkshire wicketkeeper Jonathan Tattersall is a story of redemption and second chances, having been released in 2015, but catching the eye sufficiently in second-team cricket to earn an initial one-year deal for 2018.

I'm about to ask why this young fan is so enamoured with one of the lower-profile Yorkshire county cricketers when debutant Josh Poysden appears, the Warwickshire leg-spinner who signed a three-year deal for Yorkshire in time to make his home debut at North Marine Road this year. He's the first out of the changing room to signal the half-hour, post-match debriefing is finally concluded.

Our young fan, let's call him Thomas, has his pen out and he politely asks if Josh will scribble his name down.

'Sure. As you asked so nicely,' comes the reply.

This must be the bit of a professional cricketer's job that lifts the spirits after a crushing defeat. I imagine they want to get home and forget about the match for a time, but to be sought after and appreciated can't hurt either.

Later, I spoke with Josh Poysden to get a player's view of being on the pitch at Scarborough during the Festival.

'I'd driven up from Birmingham – I've got a bit of a fear of being late – I got there nice and early. Going into the changing rooms and seeing the honours board with the list of players who've got hundreds or 5-fers, there's legends on there. Being a Yorkshire player, it was really exciting, putting you in touch with the past and the great history of the club.'

This wasn't his first match in a Yorkshire shirt. He was brought in on a one-match loan for the July Roses fixture in the County Championship, away at Old Trafford. It was recognition that without Adil Rashid, who had only committed to white-ball cricket, Yorkshire felt they needed to strengthen that area.

The alternatives at the time were off-spinner Azeem Rafiq and left-armer Karl Carver. In the end, it was Joe Root's off-spin (four wickets for five runs) that helped seal a 118-run victory for the visitors. Poysden trapped Dane Vilas lbw in an otherwise quiet debut.

He returned to action for Warwickshire and caught the eye in the T20s for Birmingham Bears before signing a contract for Yorkshire, initially on loan until the end of 2018.

Without any time to gel with his new White Rose team-mates, Poysden had to rely on the anecdotes he'd already heard about Scarborough. Apparently, a story did the rounds in the Warwickshire changing room involving

Jonathan Trott and a seagull. I could find no reference to this, so ended up imagining my own version with him either clonking one with a cover drive or a passing bird making his whites even whiter, if you get my gist.

What we don't get to see or hear about is what's said behind closed doors. So, after the defeat, what was the tone and mood during Yorkshire's subsequent lock-in at the North Marine Road changing room? Don't expect Poysden, or anyone else for that matter, to spill trade secrets, but he does lift the lid a little.

'The standards that Yorkshire as a county and club set; we knew we were quite far short. We talked through that. I always think if you just spray (criticise) everyone, you're not really going to get that much out of it, better if you can talk honestly, openly and productively about how you're going to improve.'

Thinking of Thomas, we touch on the importance of giving autographs at the end of the game and talking to fans, even through the tough times.

'I think that whatever happens, whether you have an amazing win or get absolutely smashed, it's really important to be consistent and make sure that you give back to the fans and members. That's a no-brainer. We're so lucky and privileged to be playing professional cricket, and specifically at Yorkshire, it's important you do the right things.'

Back when I was young Thomas's age, I collected stamps from my local garage (based on how much petrol my dad bought) because you could save up and exchange them for prizes. This was invariably low-grade tat that you'd only want in your home if planning a 99p garage sale. Never mind that my father had purchased thousands of pounds of petrol so that I could get a crystal glass that weighed as much as a tank and was best donated to a skip.

Rarely have I been so earnestly dedicated to anything in my life than collecting those coupons and it started a bit of a phase. For a time, I became a philatelist and would know my Penny Black from the classic charcoal 75p postage stamp of the 1980s, not that I ever found the former lurking in the bags of stamps I'd bought from a High Street shop in Taunton.

However, cricket soon took over and the obsession of collecting signatures was the new focus. Luminaries such as Hampshire bowler Cardigan Connor or Somerset's run machine Jimmy Cook were sought after and I kept a meticulous record that would eclipse my future GCSE and A-Level exams.

I can see the appeal of collecting signatures in the same way that I understand why someone would find satisfaction in scoring a county game and keeping it as a snapshot in time.

To lead you back to North Marine Road, Thomas is doing a fine job of scooping up all the Yorkshire players' signatures, one by one, as they gradually collect up their kit and step out. While clearly the result and performance at Scarborough was a long way short of what was expected, this is a side to county players many fans don't get to see.

Either by following online or seeing a game and then

swiftly heading for the exit to beat the traffic, many miss the full picture of the professionalism that caught my attention at the end of the 132nd Scarborough Cricket Festival.

The Yorkshire players sign bats or programmes, pose for group photos and summon up a smile for the twenty-first century's version of the stamp collection: the selfie. You could argue it's their job. You could grumble that it's the least they could do after a home result that was embarrassing. All I know is that for Thomas, and others who had waited patiently for their heroes to appear, it mattered and would long be remembered.

Mick, dressing room attendant at Yorkshire, is up on the pavilion balcony. He slowly, reverentially, lowers the Yorkshire flag with a face of concentration or sobriety, I can't tell. It takes a while as it flaps in the breeze, but carefully comes down and is folded. There's a poignancy and an obvious symbolism to each tug as the Yorkshire White Rose resists, quietens and is subdued.

David Willey has a photo with the admirably persistent Thomas, walks away and pauses before asking the young lad to follow the England all-rounder into the home changing room. Thomas returns to his family, beaming, with Willey's Yorkshire Vikings cap and a pair of Tim Bresnan's spikes.

We need young cricket fans to be connecting with the county game at a time when the County Championship feels threatened and relegated to the least popular margins of the season. Four days in whites may not be the format that electrifies them at first, but these touch points can start a connection to cricket that can last a lifetime.

So many of the onlookers that I talked to had been coming to the Festival since childhood or for many years. Scarborough has a magnetic pull all of its own and we shouldn't underestimate its ability to inspire a loyalty that competes with Snapchat or a computer game.

Moeen Ali walks past and is politely collared for a photo by a lady clutching an iPad. He has had a satisfying week and Scarborough has amplified the calls for a return to Test cricket as only eight wickets and a double hundred in three days can.

* * *

I leave Scarborough Cricket Club, lingering for one last look, turn left and follow North Marine Road to the corner for a final meal in North Bay Cafe which is noticeably quiet now that the cricket is over. I take a window seat and spy an ornament: a wooden yacht with 'Gentle Sea' written onto its sail. As several Yorkshire players walk past with their kit, it strikes me that the squad are seeking to ride out the storm, but right now find themselves in particularly choppy waters.

Funny where your mind wanders off to. The phrase, 'It will all come out in the wash,' is turning over in my head like the laundrette towards the other end of North Marine Road with the cheeky but practical sign in the window to 'drop your pants here.'

It being lunchtime, apple crumble and custard is the order of the day. It arrives as a fruity, glistening castle surrounded by a yellow moat and is perfect. On a whim, Mrs Fuller and I decide to test the crazy golf course down Peasholm Road, just opposite the Bowls Centre. It has seen better days, could do with a lick of paint and some Polyfilla, but forget the Ryder Cup; give me cannons, lighthouses and ships to negotiate every day of the week.

I start with a hole-in-one, but also take 15 shots on par seven as my approach rebounds off a cannon ball that I bet Danny Willett doesn't have to contend with on the PGA European Tour. We hack our way round, collapsing in laughter. A family are so enthralled at our dubious skills that they come and sit on a park bench to watch us.

The chalkboard at the entrance notes that Callum shot 46, the lowest round of the day and we are a mere 18 shots off usurping him. We add our scores for posterity and make our way down to Royal Albert Drive with a view to walking around the headland to Scarborough's South Bay.

A gentleman sits on a bench gazing out to sea. His walking stick is in his left hand and the crook of his right arm is casually resting on the back of the bench with his hand hanging down. He wears a flat cap and a long overcoat that goes most of the way to his ankles. The left lapel is open, perhaps caught in the breeze.

As we approach, his head is tilted down in thought with his right leg stretched out. It looks as if it's a regular place to spend time by the sea and ponder his life. This is the super-sized sculpture called Freddie Gilroy and the Belsen

Stragglers, some eight feet tall, made from rusting steel by artist Ray Lonsdale.

The piece itself is arresting, but the story behind it and how it came to be a permanent Scarborough landmark is just as powerful. It is based on the ex-soldier Gilroy, part of the British 11th Armoured Division who liberated the Bergen-Belsen concentration camp on April 15, 1945.

Freddie had his 24th birthday during his time at the camp and the horrors would remain with him for the rest of his life, moved to tears each year as he officially got a year older and thoughts returned to Germany.

The sculpture was initially loaned to the town for a month by the artist Lonsdale, but a public campaign to buy it in 2011 was successful. Resident Maureen Robinson stumped up her life savings of £50,000 to buy it outright and gift it to Scarborough, so here Freddie stays.

On the one hand, it is a war memorial, but also a reminder of how ordinary people had their lives turned upside down by conflict. Gilroy's life was indelibly scarred by what he saw in the Second World War and yet through the generosity of a pensioner, the town and its visitors have a piece of art that will outlive any of us.

We sit on the giant bench and I look up at Freddie; overlapping steel sheets giving his face the contours that reflect his age and the burdens that are plain to see, mouth arched down in disturbed reflection. I can't tell you when I first became fond of statues. It's not an overnight obsession, more of a gradual appreciation.

Scarborough could do with a statue to reflect the role

that the Scarborough Cricket Festival has had on the town since 1876, but not in the ground itself. It should be somewhere prominent, as Freddie is, to become a talking point for non-cricket fans.

We wave goodbye to the latest addition to my shortlist of favourite statues (alongside the 'Angel of the North' and also 'Another Place' by Antony Gormley, the installation dotted across Crosby Beach) and stroll the mile or so with the grey wall of the North Sea on our left.

Just as our feet are complaining, the ferris wheel on Marine Drive signals the start of Scarborough Harbour. Past souvenir shops, amusement arcades and fish and chips outlets is The Waterfront Cafe, a prime location to sip a tea, set back from the noise and bustle, but with the glass frontage opened out for some alfresco gawping.

* * *

The return leg is cooler, being that it is late afternoon and the wind has got up. We pass numerous dog owners, with tiny pooches striding purposefully along, noses snuffling at anything and everything. In the water, a pod of dolphins are close enough to shore to see their bodies breach the surface a few times, with the arch of dorsal fins poking out like a submarine's telescope.

If I'm being honest, Yorkshire's capitulation has left a lingering sense of, well, what is it exactly? Mostly frustration that the Scarborough adventure came to such an unsatisfactory end. It's as if I have built a sandcastle I've been looking forward to constructing all year, only to see it wiped out as the tide comes in early.

Does a bruising defeat puncture the holiday bonhomie? Those cricket fans I asked on the last day were putting a brave face on it, determined to have a final knees-up in town before the journey home.

Worcestershire's innings and 186-run victory was the largest margin of innings defeat ever inflicted on Yorkshire at North Marine Road. Could the county bounce back and stave off relegation? At that moment, I didn't much care. I wanted to hold onto Scarborough for a bit longer, so we stood, entranced at the dolphins, a final treat to send us on our way.

It's a wrap

For those who love their stats or like to take a trip down memory lane, here's how the rest of the 2018 season unfolded.

Moeen Ali is picked for the last two Tests of England's summer and claims 12 wickets overall, as well as being promoted to number three and notching a fifty at the Kia Oval as India lose by 118 runs. The 'Scarborough effect' on Yorkshire is less of a fairy tale, although it might ultimately have had a say in turning their fortunes around.

Being thrashed at home by the team at the foot of the County Championship table is a low point. Players, staff and fans returned to Headingley for the visit of Somerset wanting to put things right. The ensuing defeat by 224 runs did nothing to stem the anxiety, but there were still four games to reverse their fortunes.

The trip to Trent Bridge to face Nottinghamshire was arguably more of a defining moment of the 2018 season. The hosts racked up 448 all out and the sense of déjà vu was overwhelming. Instead, Gary Ballance (104) then Tom Kohler-Cadmore (with his first hundred for his county in red-ball cricket), led Yorkshire to 498, all five batting bonus points and a welcome draw.

The match breathes new life into Yorkshire and the victory over Lancashire by 95 runs at Headingley in September had a real sense of do-or-die about it. Tom Kohler-Cadmore and Gary Ballance finished the season with a batting flourish and Jack Brooks' performances reminded everyone what will be missed, now he has signed for Somerset.

For a format where games last four days and scheduling appears to do its level best to confuse and deflate enthusiasm, the County Championship delivers late-season drama every year. With every single point appreciatively savoured, Yorkshire bagged a rain-affected draw with Hampshire at Headingley to all but guarantee survival. Not a word anyone associated with Yorkshire County Cricket Club aims for, but when the chips are down, staving off relegation is a victory in itself.

Players much maligned on social media ('That Bresnan, how's ee got a blooming two-year contract?') step forward to do the business. Tim Bresnan's 5-28 and Adam Lyth's 134 not out are performances against Hampshire from stalwarts who have had a quiet year by their own standards.

Having been eviscerated at Scarborough, there was a sense of the wheel turning full circle when Yorkshire travelled to face Worcestershire at New Road for the final game of the 2018 season, still requiring two points to stay up.

By then, it was confirmed that Worcestershire would start 2019 in Division Two after losing to Essex by an innings and 129 runs at Chelmsford. Yorkshire duly claimed the six wickets needed to get them two bowling bonus points on the first day. Cue a massive sigh of relief.

As with the Scarborough Cricket Festival, Daryl Mitchell did score another hundred (127) but Moeen Ali was out for a breezy 60 this time as Worcestershire managed 340 all out. It was a credible first innings score at that time of year and Yorkshire needed to get their heads down, apply themselves, drop anchor, you get the gist.

September brought with it some stunning scorecards, even for seasoned county cricket aficionados who think they've seen it all. The tied match between Lancashire and Somerset at Taunton stood out as a particular marvel with Lancashire out for 99 in their first innings and Somerset set 78 to win, but dismissed for 77, having been 37-6 at one point.

Back in Worcester, Yorkshire's 428 all out off 90.5 overs laid any doubt to rest that they were striding across the finishing line rather than stumbling across it, red-faced and wheezing. Gary Ballance had an eventful season, to put it mildly. Beginning as captain, choosing to hand over the reins to Steve Patterson in June and ending with a bang that saw him finish with 906 Championship runs.

Again, he was the backbone of a run chase that saw Yorkshire win by seven wickets and finish the County Championship in fourth place. Seamer Jack Brooks signed off in style and concluded his time at Yorkshire with two County Championship titles, 316 first-class wickets and a top score of 106 not out against Lancashire.

The end of October brought with it the news that the

County Championship was moving to 10 teams in Division One from 2020. It means that 2019 is a transition year with only one side being relegated and three Division Two teams being promoted.

Making Division One top-heavy can be interpreted as more security for the top tier sides, undoubtedly true as it is that those counties currently in Division Two have more opportunity to be promoted.

In the short-term, there is less chance of relegation, but the flip side of this is more meaningless games in the top flight from 2020 where sides will neither be champions nor slipping down the trapdoor. The County Championship has delivered riveting action, right down to the wire, for years and while I know why this change has happened, doesn't it water down the permutations that kept fans enthralled?

I did a double-take at the confirmation from the ECB that the 50-over One-Day Cup would run alongside the new competition. Or put another way, they will compete directly with each other for attention and attendance. I've muttered about this more than once before, but it strikes me as counter-intuitive. The fear from the 10 counties not part of the new competition must surely be that the limited-overs festival of cricket they're still connected to will wither on the vine.

My other bugbear is that it makes plenty of assumptions. I'm not privy to market research, but it seems that the same demographic of cricket fans currently paying out for the T20 Blast will be expected to dip in their pockets a second time. I've noticed that I vacillate between pretending not to care about the ever-changing county game and being extremely opinionated and feeling a sense of ownership.

On which note, the revelation that overseas players will not be allowed in the One-Day Cup drew a laboured sigh that reverberated around the office. I wish we'd make up our mind. Are overseas players good or bad for the professional game in this country?

Ok, it might not be as binary as that, but it feels like a muddled rationale. We'll use the One-Day Cup to encourage home-grown talent to thrive, but starve it of the quality and diversity that will help English and Welsh cricketers improve. I don't know about you, but I'd happily watch Matt Waite take on Aaron Finch in 50-over cricket.

When the Scarborough Cricket Festival was in its pomp, overseas players were at the heart of its appeal and it worries me that we have one competition looming that will actively seek to draw Virat Kohli and others to our shores and another, with the rest of the counties in it, that will shut the door on overseas admissions. Apparently, there was unanimous support for this, so if it ends up encouraging domestic players and allowing them more game-time, that's to be applauded, though I wouldn't have done it.

But let's not dwell on the machinations of the domestic game for too long and look forward instead to the year ahead in all its glory. For Yorkshire, that will mean hosting four ICC World Cup matches in June and July, including England against Sri Lanka.

I wonder to what extent World Cup fever grips the country or not? We welcome England, Sri Lanka, Pakistan,

Afghanistan, West Indies and India during the tournament up in Yorkshire, and it will be as much about the events and buzz around clubs and communities as what takes place on the field.

Personally, one of the highlights of the year has to be the third Specsavers Ashes Test Match in August at Emerald Headingley. It's long overdue that this historic rivalry returns to Yorkshire. What are the odds of persuading the Aussies to stay on a bit after their tour officially ends in September and bolt on a game at Scarborough, for old times' sake?

Reading the tea leaves

It's late January 2019 and I'm pulling my thoughts together on the Festival, toggling between the Word document on my computer and England's attempts to save the First Test in Barbados. Joe Root has just been dismissed with a vicious bouncer, but it was a massive no-ball by Shannon Gabriel.

There's much to ponder since the end of the 2018 County Championship and it inevitably revolves around the machinations of the fixtures and what they mean for Yorkshire County Cricket Club and Scarborough Cricket Club.

Surrey in June and Nottinghamshire in August will be the respective visitors to North Marine Road in 2019, with York Cricket Club taking its first-ever County Championship fixture at Clifton Park. There has only been one first-class match in York, but you have to turn back time to June 9, 1890, at Wigginton Road, now a dormant field next to a railway crossing and the B1363.

It's unquestionably the case that outgrounds will see more county matches in future as a by-product of the new 100-ball, city-based competition inked in for 2020. As my fingers clatter across the keyboard in a pair of my wife's fetching pink fingerless gloves, I still don't know any more than you do.

The teams and these rules are being thrashed out behind closed doors but, in the context of the Scarborough Cricket Festival, the exact shade of crimson lycra the cricket kit will come in matters less than there being Yorkshire home games across formats up for grabs, where once it was all locked down.

This year is something of a dress rehearsal, albeit for different reasons. Outgrounds have become fashionable again at counties hosting World Cup games. Hampshire head for the Isle of Wight, Middlesex travel to Radlett and Glamorgan return to Newport for the first time in half a century.

It is with the lemony tang of irony that because of an alleged appetite for an entirely new form of the game, English cricket is actually going back to the way things used to be.

Some have interpreted York's addition to the County Championship fixture list as a snub to Scarborough. But was it more about spreading county cricket further afield? The man who could definitively answer that question was Mark Arthur, Yorkshire County Cricket Club's Chief Executive.

When Arthur was appointed to the role in May 2013, the county had been without a Chief Executive since Stewart Regan moved to the Scottish Football Association three years earlier. Did he know how big a deal cricket at Scarborough was to the region?

When Mark was Chief Executive of Nottinghamshire County Cricket Club, Nottinghamshire came to Scarborough in 1996 for an AXA Equity and Law League game. The visitors were pushing for the title and the visit made quite the impression.

'I came up here with my wife and very young son. We sat down at the bottom end of the ground; he was in his pushchair. We watched Chris Cairns hitting sixes over mid-on and wide extra cover for fun. The crowd must have been eight or nine thousand. I was very much aware what Scarborough had to offer from a cricketing perspective.'

Of course, we don't know where our careers will take us, but in Arthur's case, after county cricket came 13 years at Nottingham Forest Football Club before Colin Graves' move to become deputy chairman of the ECB precipitated a vacancy at Headingley.

As you'd expect for a Chief Executive, Mark's measured with what he says, acutely aware that anything can be seized upon and misinterpreted. Heading up a county club of the size and scope of Yorkshire comes with stakeholders numbering tens of thousands.

In Yorkshire, we're not backward in coming forward when it comes to strongly-held views on county cricket. It's part of what attracted me to move here myself, but for Arthur there is a balancing act between celebrating all that Scarborough is and does with wider issues affecting Yorkshire County Cricket Club.

'I understood how important the Festival was to supporters, members and players and that it had a significant role to play in the history of Yorkshire County Cricket Club and going forward.

'From my point of view, I soon got caught up in Scarborough fever and I'm a massive fan of what it delivers. I don't go there these days just as the Chief Executive of Yorkshire County Cricket Club. I go there because I enjoy the atmosphere, the cricket it produces and the pitch John Dodds prepares is so quick that there's always something going on. The players love playing there. Apart from that final match at Lord's in 2016, it will always generate the largest first and second-day crowds (and the aggregate crowd) for any County Championship match in the country in a single year.'

We all have our preferred vantage points at North Marine Road. For Mark, he prefers to sit up in the first-floor Scarborough offices by the entrance where he can survey everything. He admits to being a people-watcher and likes to see what's going on, people enjoying themselves and their interactions.

But, I hear you ask, where will Scarborough Cricket Club fit into Yorkshire's plans over the next ten years? The answer is encouraging, but comes with certain caveats. My timing is impeccable. The England & Wales Cricket Board had just announced its strategic plan for the next five years and that impacts what the Scarborough Cricket Festival will look like.

'As far as I'm concerned, it's business as usual. We would expect that from 2020 to 2024, we now know exactly what cricket is going to be played. We know that there will be four 50-over games which cannot be played at Emerald Headingley while the new competition is being played there. Two of those are likely to be at Scarborough.'

On the surface, that would address concerns voiced by Scarborough Cricket Club and Yorkshire fans that the Festival has shrunk and feels a little precarious, especially when you factor in the weather or games finishing days before they're meant to. Yorkshire have listened and the new 100-ball competition, love it or hate it, has meant there is now a little flex in the calendar to further support outgrounds.

'That brings them (Scarborough) back to the ten days that they need to sustain a business capable of hosting first-class cricket. We're very cognisant of that, as in the last few years, they haven't had ten days because of the change to the structure of the County Championship. We had to split the days that we lost and we've seen the pain that caused their club. Hopefully from 2020 to 2024, we can get back to business as usual.'

For supporters of Scarborough, that's an important first step. Yet, the competing priorities of counties and the annual unknown that is the fixture list mean there are still questions and ones that can't necessarily be answered as tidily as we'd like.

If North Marine Road is the beneficiary of two 50-over games from 2020, it remains to be seen how popular they are. There are all sorts of nuances at play here. For a start, the typical audience to the Scarborough Cricket Festival is not the same as a crowd for a limited-overs thrash. You might reasonably counter that in the Festival of old, when it was ten or more days linked together, one-day crowds were enormous.

Ah, but when will those 50-over matches at Scarborough happen? Will they be in a block as part of an enlarged Festival or scattered randomly? To my mind, it makes sense to try to schedule them as part of the Festival rather than dotted about in any given summer, but that would have to be requested by Yorkshire and they may have more important considerations when it comes to ranking what goes where.

Then, there is the prickly pear of selection, if the 50-over game runs concurrently with the new 100-ball competition. I know we're straying into wild speculation, but such points of order come with real-life consequences for Scarborough Cricket Club.

They will be different beasts, but it's inconceivable that one will not dominate the other. If The Hundred is as successful as the powers that be would like, it will grow as the Indian Premier League and Big Bash have done. That needs space and something will have to give, or else we'll have to start in February or end in October, much to the chagrin of county groundsmen.

There are many moving parts, none of which I'm party to, yet the point around selection makes for awkward reading. Will crowd attendances still blossom if a Yorkshire XI is diluted with half its first-team missing? The flip-side is more game-time for fringe players and new stars emerging.

An area of potential growth at Scarborough is other prestige games, besides men's county matches, and Arthur sees women's cricket as a fitting companion on the next leg of its evolution.

'We have encouraged the ECB, and they have responded, to give Scarborough Cricket Club some extra matches so they have Diamonds matches and England Women. That is going to develop quite a bit as women's cricket becomes more professionalised. At the moment, there's only 22 professional women, but that will go up to roughly 100 from 2020, so the opportunity is very much there.'

Thoughts turned to the battleground for Yorkshire's outgrounds. In the last couple of years, there has been talk of Bradford and Sheffield hosting List A or first-class cricket in future, but that seems unlikely any time soon – because of limited games available and both sites requiring upgrades.

At this stage, Scarborough has no competition as the first-choice outground for Yorkshire County Cricket Club, but the question for Mark has to be: why didn't Scarborough get that third match in 2019, preferring instead to give it to York?

'First of all, it costs us a lot of money as a club to go to Scarborough. There are hotel and travel costs, not only for players but also staff who go over there. The hotels in Scarborough are some of the most expensive in the country when they obviously take advantage of the cricket, which sticks in my throat a little bit, because the only reason they can charge those prices is because the cricket's turning up – yet the cricket is having to pay quite large amounts of money.'

You might raise an eyebrow at that, given Yorkshire's own prices are hiked for an India one-day international or an Ashes Test. It's classic supply and demand, though we mustn't forget that Mark's remit is to balance the books at a county club currently some £24m in debt.

Arthur's argument against giving Scarborough a third County Championship fixture (and temporarily topping up their allowance to 12 days a year) is partly concern over watering down the Scarborough X-factor.

'There's the question of whether we'd be spreading an existing audience across three games rather than two; whether that may have reduced the uniqueness of Scarborough's appeal.'

It might sound odd for the author of a book cherishing the enchantment of cricket by the sea to agree, but if there's a chance to also take county cricket to Bradford and Sheffield in the next decade, I think we should grab it.

It's 49 miles via the A171 between Middlesbrough and Scarborough, a further 47 miles South to Hull and 38 miles between Sheffield and Headingley. Not insurmountable distances, but not down the road either. How far would you travel to watch a game of cricket?

The scale of Yorkshire, if we're imagining it's one geographical entity for a moment, is enormous. At nearly 12,000 square kilometres and over 5 million people, it is both opportunity and headache for those governing cricket.

Under Arthur, Yorkshire have made a conscious effort to reconnect with supporters across the land by taking T20 warm-up matches to Hull, Middlesbrough, Bradford, Harrogate and York.

The clarion call by Yorkshire County Cricket Club is: we're not just Leeds-centric; a view backed by the work done at grassroots by Arthur and the first-team squad who tour clubs in winter and take part in question-and-answer sessions for cricket societies from Cottingham to Barnsley.

As for York Cricket Club, they've gradually won over the county club since representative games have been going to Clifton Park in the past decade. It hasn't hurt their cause that York has the second-highest density of Yorkshire members after Leeds.

'During our travels, York have done a tremendous job in the T20 warm-up games, benefit games, Yorkshire Diamonds matches and second-eleven matches. They have quality facilities that means with a little bit of extra support, we're able to take first-class cricket there in 2019 – which is likely to be a one-off. These are exceptional circumstances and York will also benefit from having List A cricket in 2020 and 2021.'

The ten-year staging agreement between Yorkshire County Cricket Club and Scarborough Cricket Club that was signed in 2010 expires this year, and I'd expect that to be formally renewed by the time of the Nottinghamshire game in August.

Mark Arthur elaborated further, specifying it will be a five-year deal this time, based on the strategic vision of the national governing body, the ECB, running to 2024.

'Because we've seen the complexity and changing face (of domestic county cricket), the deal will go until 2024 where we have certainty of cricket. Everything depends on the cricket that the ECB wants us to deliver.

'It would be wrong to give a long-term contract to anybody. We don't have a long-term contract with the ECB, except we're a shareholder. We have certainty of cricket here until 2024 and quite simply, any future deal at Scarborough will mirror what we've got.'

At first reading, that might sound more ominous than it is. Cricket at Scarborough is only guaranteed for five years, but then just as county cricket at Headingley won't evaporate overnight, neither will it do so at North Marine Road.

It's unthinkable that there won't be a Scarborough Cricket Festival for many decades to come. If the County Championship is eroded in time, however, it might become the sole men's county match at Scarborough.

* * *

I guess we can all debate as to the best future course of action for Scarborough, but one point of view I hadn't heard before was around the timing of the Festival. It's a theme that has cropped up a few times, but a conversation with Sir Gary Verity, Chief Executive of Welcome to Yorkshire at the time, gave a different slant.

Heading up the tourism body for Yorkshire meant he

regularly saw the benefits, but also the untapped potential of the Scarborough Cricket Festival.

'It is accurately described as the oldest and greatest cricket Festival in the world. It's a great asset, not just for Scarborough, but I would argue even wider than Yorkshire, for the whole of the country.'

Ok, so far, so on point. But Verity thinks it shouldn't be in August at all.

'The only thing that's important for the Festival is to make sure it gets the respect it deserves in terms of fixture placement. It's crazy that we can't get the scheduling right. The Festival has been in September and it's crept further forwards into August – and Scarborough is busy in August anyway.

'Putting it into September, just before the kids go back to school is certainly the time to do that, it helps stretch the season.'

The rationale for that is the Scarborough Cricket Festival has clashed in recent years with other big events in the county, such as the Ebor Festival at York Racecourse. Tricky, not least because Welcome to Yorkshire sponsors both, but I don't know to what extent county cricket attendees and racegoers overlap.

If we turn our attention back to the actual cricket, it's not so long ago that Scarborough was a fortress for Yorkshire County Cricket Club and, just before this book nipped off to the publishers, I sat down with Director of Cricket, Martyn Moxon, to get to grips with how that's so dramatically changed.

The 2018 Festival defeat against Worcestershire was particularly striking in that a team battling for relegation thumped Yorkshire so convincingly. There's never one reason for a defeat, but Martyn's take is that it all began at the toss and went downhill from there (my words, not his). Certainly the absence of Steve Patterson and Ben Coad gave the bowling attack a less experienced look, but momentum can be hard to claw back too.

'You don't want to make excuses, but the toss makes a big difference. Because it's such a good cricket pitch, there's good pace, bounce and carry. If there's anything in it for the seamers, it's really tough that first morning. We were a little bit low on confidence from a batting perspective. We had a couple of unfortunate dismissals and once we were bowled out for a lowish total, I think we saw in Daryl Mitchell and Moeen Ali, two batsmen that had a point to prove. They were scrapping for their lives at the bottom of the table. They played unbelievably well. We found it really tough.'

Typically, cricket at Scarborough has proven to be an occasion that acts as a catalyst, either to confirm a team's belief in its capacity to win a title or cement the notion of a side heading for another Division. It wasn't the case last year as Yorkshire got their act together in time, as Moxon acknowledged.

'It was a bad defeat for us, probably made worse because of the position in the table we were in at that time, but the pleasing thing for me was how we recovered from that. Ultimately, Worcestershire got relegated and we didn't. It was a bad game, they played well, we didn't. It was made a lot of because of the circumstances of being beaten so comprehensively by a team below us.'

I've kicked around the topic of county cricket's scheduling at some length, but usually from the point of view of the fan or the host club. Naturally, it has consequences for a county club looking to win games and prepare in the best way possible too. For Yorkshire and Moxon, coming to terms with Scarborough's surface needs a re-think.

'The point about Scarborough is that we have to find a way of winning there again. A lot of it is us batting better and coping with the bounce. We've got to get our next generation of batsmen used to that because there aren't that many surfaces around like it now. We've spoken about it with Andrew Gale to try and spend a bit more time in preparation at Scarborough.'

Yorkshire County Cricket Club have since appointed Paul Grayson as full-time batting coach, but the point about allowing more time to get ready for a fixture is entirely in the hands of, guess what, the schedule.

It will be impossible to head to the coast earlier this August as Yorkshire Vikings play Durham Jets on the Friday at Headingley, travel to Scarborough on the Saturday with the Festival's Championship game against Nottinghamshire starting on the Sunday.

However, for the earlier June match against Surrey at North Marine Road, Yorkshire finish at York against Warwickshire on the 20th and don't play at Scarborough until the 30th – allowing a longer acclimatisation.

It's now the way of things, from clubs to counties to internationals, but I have a bee in my bonnet about switching of formats. Coaches and players will say it's just part and parcel of the modern game, but it can't help preparation if you've been aiming to hit every ball for six into Headingley the night before trying to bat all day at Scarborough.

* * *

ESPNcricinfo's UK Editor David Hopps is one who sees North Marine Road's lifespan inextricably linked with the relative health of the County Championship and fluctuations based on the indomitable rise of shorter formats.

'I'm optimistic for Scarborough if county cricket holds together, but I'm worried about county cricket. There's a move away from Championship cricket. The future could be a stitch-up between the top eight counties. I like T20, but I'm very uncomfortable with some of the things I'm seeing.'

His view speaks to an ongoing landslide that will reshape English cricket. 'I think it's a massively uncertain time for the game. If the county game's under threat, and if we have to deliver the sort of product India wants, rather than what English cricket fans want, because of TV rights money, then I think we're in a very dicey time.

'When I retire, I want to spend my time in the summer

watching county cricket and I'm not fully confident I'll see a fixture list I'm totally happy with.'

As something of a snap poll on Facebook, a social media platform known for serious discussion, I asked my *CricketYorkshire.com* audience what the Scarborough Cricket Festival will look like in 20 years' time. My favourite answer is this, which speaks to the subtle nuances of the global game:

'15 x 100-ball games, 10 x T20s and a 50-over pink and yellow spotted ball game starting at 11pm with the players in mankinis. It's the ECB way.'

A penny for your own thoughts on the subject. Not the mankinis. Unless it's a blazing hot day then that's just asking for trouble and possibly hyperthermia.

I note the level of animosity aimed at cricket's governing body for England and Wales that crops up online frequently. We all feel like we could run the game, our game, more competently, but there does seem to be consistent protests, or perhaps they're just the squeaky wheels. Is it the same in every sport?

There is certainly deep concern echoing David's views about what the County Championship will look like in future decades. I'd go so far to say that there is a disconnect, that fans don't feel represented or heard.

So, where does the Scarborough Cricket Festival sit in all of this? On the one hand, its heritage and current popularity offer some guarantee of longevity. Yet, as others have noted, Scarborough is only as safe as the length and breadth of the County Championship. The bigger question is whether a format that attracts relatively few spectators and is rarely televised can survive in anything like its present state over the next 20 or 30 years.

How about this? It is 2044. The T5 Super Series, sponsored by blinkandyoumissit.com, is coming to a close in Leeds after 647 matches. We are into December and the Scarborough Cricket Show is up next at North Marine Road which is a venue for a night of ice-cricket with the English game now 365 days-a-year.

My glimpse into a dystopian future that, fingers crossed, never comes to pass is not entirely without merit. Immediate popularity only stretches so far and if the tide turns wholeheartedly towards bite-sized formats then that will define cricket in the next half a century.

It partly depends if you believe that T20 is now the gateway to a lifetime passion for cricket in the same way that so many people referenced an experience at Scarborough as being the hook for them.

I'd like to think that our tastes evolve over time and, much in the same way that I woke one day to the sudden realisation that I had become a Radio 4 listener, so too we might clutch to the notion that those younger generations, pigeonholed with a micro attention span, will find their cricketing appetites change too.

As we all age, the more entrenched our views become because we've worked out what we like and know our minds. We also like to take our time too, savouring a Test match that lasts five days (if you can find one) as if it were a maturing Cheddar or a ripening Cabernet Sauvignon.

The Office for National Statistics projects that by 2066, there will be 5.1 million people aged 85 years and over, roughly 7% of the total UK population. By then, will they be infused and enthused by ever decreasing durations of cricket? Are we destined to get to a point where we'll need three cricketers to bowl a ball like some weird sporting mime?

Conversely, those teens now following Yorkshire Vikings and revelling in fireworks and a booming sound system between overs might graduate to munching chips in the North Stand at Scarborough and delighting in the number of dot balls between lunch and tea intervals.

Doom-mongers have long been predicting the demise of the County Championship, but it is still here and still the one that matters above all else. Nor should we demonise T20 and its offshoots. The potential of the Festival is to bring both formats together again and introduce younger audiences to the magic of cricket at Scarborough.

I'm of the mind that nothing should be ruled out. On the one hand, the sheer joy of watching cricket at North Marine Road is that it doesn't change too much. It's not a stretch to imagine how it would have been when Don Bradman walked out to bat.

Yet, we're on the brink of major changes in the county game and Scarborough needs to stay relevant and unforgettable. Could introducing short-form cricket bring new audiences to an expanded Festival?

For now, let's savour the Scarborough Cricket Festival as it is. There's nothing better than to walk the ground and take it all in. The gentleman in the red beret by the tea room, one eye on the cricket while sucking his teeth at a taxing sudoku puzzle in the paper. The row of mobility scooters tucked away behind the sight screen at the Trafalgar Square entrance, ready for a motorised dash to the chippy.

The boy in white cricket shirt, clutching a blue plastic bat, driving his mum's bowling into the sea of legs on the outfield at lunch. A swaying tower of pale yellow takeaway boxes staggering past, with hairy arms hugging the precious cargo.

Let's end as we began with my green Scarborough ticket stub. It hasn't aged a day since a steward casually passed it over on the gate years ago. Therein lies the essence of what the Scarborough Cricket Festival delivers.

It's a time capsule, an oasis, an antidote to life's pressures, a gentle passing of time, a place for new friendships and those spanning decades, where the best marriage of relaxation by the sea and world-class cricket meet.

Acknowledgements

The decision to write a cricket book is the easy bit. It's like buying a new house. You go round, get swept up in the excitement on the first viewing then return with the tape measure to work out if the fish tank and the flat-screen TV will fit.

There wasn't a eureka moment in deciding to take on the cherished cricketing heirloom that is the Scarborough Cricket Festival. It's been percolating away for a few years, but once the decision was made, a sense of responsibility not to stuff it up wasn't far behind.

Generosity plays a key part within these pages. I've relied on the time and knowledge of many people from across the world who have shared their stories, given advice or offered their expertise.

Research tentatively began with a loan of books from a friend of mine, Brian Sanderson, that included J.M. Kilburn's *Overthrows* and *Thanks to Cricket*. It gave context to how the Festival used to be and its importance to the town. I also got my hands on *Cricket at Scarborough* by Ian Hall with John Found and that provided all manner of background.

As I write this, a souvenir programme of the Asda

Cricket Challenge from 1984 is on my desk. It's an A4, full-colour reminder of the peripheral efforts around the Festival at that time. Funded by the supermarket giant, it matches any cricket magazine there is today with articles by Brian Close, Godfrey Evans, Ian Botham and Bill Bowes.

The gift of some Scarborough Cricket Club membership booklets by a Yorkshire member sparked particular joy. They are tiny pieces of cricket memorabilia (smaller than A6) that are very satisfying to hold and flick through to glean titbits from a decade or so past, so thank you to Andrew Hopkins for those.

The pale yellow dust jacket for 2006 members shows that the 120th Annual Festival included Old Yorkshire XI vs Old Lancashire XI, in aid of the Dickie Bird Foundation. Google can do many things in the blink of an eye. It cannot, however, tell me that on Wednesday September 6 at 11.30am, the British Police Cricket Club National Knockout Final took place.

The entrance tickets for Yorkshire matches included at the back are akin to the paper slips you tear to mark your place in the queue for the pharmacy or the fish counter. Each says, 'This coupon is to be surrendered at the entrance to the ground,' which delights me in many ways. The use of the word surrender conjures up in my mind a potential tug-of-war tussle.

I also have a copy of the 1986 Centenary Festival booklet written by John Herbert who, in a sign of how club cricket used to be covered, had been Yorkshire League correspondent for BBC Radio Leeds and contributor to the *Club Cricketer* magazine.

It is a gentle, intelligent read reflecting on the history of the Festival, the removal of the MCC fixture and of touring sides. John picks out his favourite year of 1953:

'If time travel would permit and I could go back and re-create for myself one Festival from the past, I would choose 1953. The Australians were in England, Everest had been climbed and a new Queen sat on the throne. At school, we were given propelling pencils with a crown on top. I used mine for my duties as scorer at Leighton Buzzard Cricket Club until the crown fell off, leaving no enclosed space to carry spare lead.'

I mention these sources in passing because the truth of it is that I hardly read any cricket books at all. Even when I'm writing one, as it turns out. My principal sources have been lots of interviews and donning flippers, snorkel and mask for a deep-dive into the furthest recesses of Google, followed by fact-checking with reliable custodians of cricket data.

It's an inevitable part of research that our memories play tricks. I have fact-checked everything as rigorously as I can, because dates, matches and people involved need anchoring down as best we can. For that, I have extensively mined the treasure that is Cricket Archive.

It is a phenomenal website offering access to 700,000 scorecards on 14,000 grounds and details of more than 1.2 million players. I must also thank Yorkshire County Cricket Club who offer a complete scoreboard archive online for free.

I have to mention someone who hitherto has not cropped up. Part of my retrospective writing was trying to piece together what actually happened on the field of play during the 2018 Festival. I have diary notes, photographs and audio files, but I was frequently yapping away, moving around the ground and often distracted from the cricket itself.

Graham Hardcastle is a prolific freelance cricket writer who can often be found running the live county blog for *The Guardian* while hammering out 1,000 words for the Yorkshire County Cricket Club website and simultaneously tweeting about Gary Ballance's fifty. Technology has brought us so much more content than ever before and Graham is one of those working feverishly to satisfy that demand.

His observations and reports from the Scarborough Cricket Festival enabled me to piece together a chronology and with any luck, give all of you a sense of place and immediacy around which I sometimes went off on a tangent. Graham, and many other journalists like him, act as the glue that underpins much of our insatiable appetite for up-to-the-second cricket news and where would we be without them?

In acknowledging all of the contributions that led to this point, it would be remiss of me not to thank Scarborough Cricket Club and Yorkshire County Cricket Club. There has been considerable support from both in all kinds of ways, from Scarborough's Rob Richtering answering my random emails on weekends about a particular point of order from over 40 years ago, to Yorkshire's Media & Content Manager, James Coldman, who facilitated county interviews at short notice.

Time is the one defining theme of this book when I think about it. Both in terms of how the Scarborough Cricket Festival has changed so much, even in a relatively short period, to the fact that so many gave theirs generously to make this book happen.

From journalists and Chief Executives to lifelong cricket fans, all shared their points of view and personal anecdotes for which I'm grateful. We've collectively added a footnote in the history of this favourite outpost of Yorkshire cricket and who can say fairer than that?

I want to acknowledge all those who aren't mentioned here either because time ran out or, for whatever reason, the fates conspired against us. This book could easily have stretched to the girth of a Yellow Pages, back when the telephone directory landing on the doormat made everything jump off tables.

I also want to thank those who make the Festival what it is, simply by being there. The atmosphere at Scarborough is part-location, part-cricket, part-seagulls, and very much the camaraderie of those who attend. If you haven't already sampled the delights or been for a while, pencil in a day off work or treat yourself to a mini-break at the coast and see why we rave about it in Yorkshire.

By parking your backside on those wooden benches, you'll also be supporting the Festival. I think there's an inherent danger with an experience as popular as the Scarborough Cricket Festival that it is thought to be immune from the slings and arrows of outrageous fortune. Let's not put that to the test, eh?

Thanks must go to my publisher, Great Northern Books, and in particular David Burrill, who was persuaded that writing about a cricket Festival at the seaside was a gamble worth taking. On a similar thread, I really appreciate everyone who has invested their money in buying a copy, particularly those who pre-ordered and, as a result, have their names included in the back of this book.

If you've done it yourself, you'll know that writing a book has its peaks and troughs, but is nigh on impossible without the collaboration of others. The editing and proofreading stages can feel like wading through treacle, just as enthusiasm is waning. It's at this juncture that friends can make the world of difference.

Author David Warner offered to look through my manuscript in January at a time when he was up to his eyes with the *Yorkshire County Cricket Club Yearbook*. The amends came back in a matter of days, two hours happily vanished over a coffee as we debated uses of quote marks and whether I should refer to Younus Khan or Younis Khan.

As a journalist, his incredible knowledge of Yorkshire County Cricket Club since the Seventies is a thing to behold and David's skill as an editor brought fresh eyes for the final push over the line.

When the idea came to me for my second cricket book, I put together an ambitious shortlist of who might write a foreword. At the top was the broadcaster, journalist and author Sir Michael Parkinson, whose knowledge of Yorkshire cricket and direct involvement in the Scarborough Cricket Festival felt like the perfect fit.

That Michael agreed to do it in the first place was very kind and our subsequent email exchanges about the goings-on in Yorkshire club cricket and the demise of Cudworth, the South Yorkshire village he played for, made for fruitful correspondence played out over months.

Last, but actually first by a country mile, is my wife Moira, who has been amazingly supportive from the moment, 'I think I'll write a book about the Scarborough Cricket Festival,' escaped my lips. As patient editor and proofreader, she now knows of Lord Londesborough, the Fenner Trophy and the Popular Bank.

Having more strings to her bow than Robin Hood, Mrs Fuller is once again entrusted with the cover design after the artwork for *All Wickets Great and Small* received rave reviews. A cricket book saturates your life and eats up evenings and weekends for months and months. I am blessed to have an incredible batting partner who has been by my side throughout this and many innings.

It feels apt to finish with J.M. Kilburn.

As I've said, I'm not a hoarder and find it therapeutic to read and appreciate a book then release it back into the wild, usually to my local charity shop that has housed a stellar cricket collection over the years.

One book has doggedly remained in my possession since I acquired it on Ebay, of all places. A worn and faded hardback with its A5-sized blue cloth cover announcing: *The Scarborough Cricket Festival* by J.M. Kilburn.

This 1948 work by the *Yorkshire Post* Cricket Correspondent, James Maurice Kilburn, is magnificent from the moment you clap eyes on it.

The silver, embossed emblem of Scarborough Cricket Club is as unblemished as the day it was stamped by the Bradford printers Yorkdale Press. The book title and author are in the club's colour of tangerine and the long, slim font is elegant and understated.

Opening it is to be greeted by endpapers the shade of a milky coffee with a floral repeat pattern and, in my copy, a black ink attribution to its owner I.G. Hogbiz (at a guess). I can't tell you at what point I began sniffing books, but its musty aroma is reassuring.

The venerated cricket journalist J.M. Kilburn bewitched generations with his reporting of Yorkshire cricket from 1934 until he retired in 1967, but his spirit lives on in the pages of my favourite book – and it was a trusty companion in writing my own.

Inspiration can be teased from every paragraph that captures Kilburn's efficiency with language and affection for the atmosphere on the coast. The famous line, oft-quoted, simply states: 'Festival cricket, as Scarborough knows it, is first-class cricket on holiday.'

Whatever the future holds for the Scarborough Cricket Festival, I trust it will always remain first-class.

Supporters of Scarborough Cricket Festival

Derek Agar
Mike Bailey
Andrew & Deirdre Bailey
Michael Bailey
Anthony Barber
Simon Barraclough
Robert Bell
Derek Best
Adam Bloomfield
Alan P Borwell
Timothy Boyes
Christopher John Bragg
Pete Brandon
Richard Brown
Douglas Burford
Phillip Burrow
Michael Carter
Roy Cass
David Comery
Ian Coxon, Durham County
   Cricket Club
Malcolm Crane
Mark Doherty
Barry Ellis
Shaun Fisher
Peter Fisher
Ian. P. Fleming
Peter Forster
David Gaunt
Kate & Steve Grace
Robert Greenwood
Bill Greenwood OBE
Robert Griffin
Dominic L Grunwell
Richard L Grunwell

Kevin Hardisty
David Hardisty
Paul Harrand
Cathy Harrison
John Heald
Helen Heald
Andrew Hinchliffe
Chris Hirst
Robin Hobbs
Brian Hoggarth
John Holborn
Richard Holdridge
Adrian Holland
Anne & Andy Hopkirk
Robert Horner
John E Howe
Helen Hoyle
Barry Hutchinson
John Hutton
Graham Hyde
Nancy Ingleby
Richard Ingleby
Neil Ives
Tony Jack
Peter Johnson
Andrew H Jones
Kevin and Jill Jones
Rob Kelly
Iain Kindness
Charles Kitching
Mark David Lawlor
James Andrew Lawson
Jeremy Lonsdale
Sir Ian Magee
Mike and Anne Mahon

Kevin Malone

Helen Marriott @ Fountains Court Residential Centre For Wellbeing

Kenneth Marshall

Anne Mathers

Steve Mayo

Paul McFarlane

Alison McLaren

Duncan McLeod

Julie Mincher

Peter Moreland

Pamela Morris

C P Murgatroyd

Ben Nattrass

Mel Neary

Barry Newton

Bob Newton

David Normanton

Sir Michael Parkinson

Geoffrey Page

Dr. David Pendleton

Stephen Pepper

Max Perry

Clive Place

Christine Powley

In memory of Brian Powley

Robert A Procter

Robert Fox Procter

Jack Quarmby

Howard Ray

Gordon Read

Neil Readman

Graham T. Reid

Rob Richtering

Lainey Robinson

Graham Robinson, Steeton CC Stalwart

Peter R. Sauntson

Mike Sayles

Brian Scanlon

Scarborough Cricket Club

George Shannon

Andrew Shaw

Richard Shutt

Alexandra V B Skinner

Ian Sleney

Roy Smith

P.A. Smith

Robert Sproston

Dennis Stockton

Stephen Stoney

Maggie Sumner

Kevin Sutcliffe

Sam Sykes

Anthony Taylor

David Neil Theaker

Ian Thompson

Rick Thompson

David, Helen & Molly Tindall

John Todd

David Town

Robert M. Town

Ben Turnbull

Peter John Turner

Nick Waddington

Clive Waddington

Tom Walgate

Martin P Walker

Colin Watson

Peter R Watson

Paul White

Peter Wildsmith

Ian Wilson

John Wilson

Thomas Yates

Who's Who of
The Yorkshire
County Cricket Club

Compiled by Paul Dyson
Foreword by Martyn Moxon

Profiles of all those 670 men
who have represented
The Yorkshire County Cricket Club

From Alfred Ackroyd to Yuvraj Singh, from Isaac Hodgson in 1863 to
Kraigg Brathwaite in 2017, this volume features profiles of all those
670 men who have represented The Yorkshire CCC by playing for its
first eleven in first-class cricket, limited-overs matches or Twenty20
games as well as the 59 who played for 'Yorkshire' prior to the official
Club's formation. Whether they played in an amazing total of 883
matches, as Wilfred Rhodes did, or whether they wore the county
colours just once – and this, surprisingly, applies to 115 players – each
and every one of them has their own place in the county's history and
the contents within.

www.greatnorthernbooks.co.uk